The Heart of a Man

The Heart of a Man

A NAVAL PILOT'S VIETNAM DIARY

By Frank Callihan Elkins

Edited by Marilyn Roberson Elkins

Naval Institute Press
Annapolis, Maryland

This book was originally published in 1973 by W. W.
Norton and Company, Inc.

The poem "Reluctance" is reprinted from *The Poetry of
Robert Frost,* edited by Edward Connery Lathem.
Copyright 1934, © 1969 by Holt, Rinehart and Winston,
Inc. Copyright © 1962 by Robert Frost. Reprinted by
permission of Henry Holt and Company, Inc.

Library of Congress Cataloging-in-Publication Data

Elkins, Frank Callihan, 1939–1966
    The heart of a man : a naval pilot's Vietnam diary /
by Frank Callihan Elkins ; edited by Marilyn Roberson
Elkins.
        p.   cm.
    Originally published: New York : Norton, [1973].
    ISBN 1-55750-224-2
    1. Vietnamese Conflict, 1961–1975—Aerial
operations, American. 2. Vietnamese Conflict, 1961–
1975—Personal narratives, American.
3. Elkins, Frank Callihan, 1939–1966 I. Elkins,
Marilyn Roberson. II. Title.
DS559.5.E43   1991
959.704'348—dc20   90-26130
                                                CIP

Printed in the United States of America on acid-free paper ∞

9   8   7   6   5   4   3   2

First printing

The names of individuals mentioned in the diary have
been changed to protect their privacy.

Reluctance

Out through the fields and the woods
    And over the walls I have wended;
I have climbed the hills of view
    And looked at the world, and descended;
I have come by the highway home,
    And lo, it is ended.

The leaves are all dead on the ground,
    Save those that the oak is keeping
To ravel them one by one
    And let them go scraping and creeping
Out over the crusted snow,
    When others are sleeping.

And the dead leaves lie huddled and still,
    No longer blown hither and thither;
The last lone aster is gone;
    The flowers of the witch hazel wither;
The heart is still aching to seek,
    But the feet question "Whither?"

Ah, when to the heart of man
    Was it ever less than a treason
To go with the drift of things,
    To yield with a grace to reason,
And bow and accept the end
    Of a love or a season?

                                    Robert Frost

Foreword

I am deeply honored that Marilyn Elkins asked that I write the foreword to *The Heart of a Man*; first, because I greatly admire Marilyn, a fellow Tennessean, for her stirring example of courage and devotion. Secondly, because although I never met Frank Elkins, I felt I knew him vicariously through discussions with Marilyn and his sterling reputation for bravery and competence as a naval aviator.

His superb diary is one of the most moving and graphic accounts of the Vietnam combat experiences of a carrier pilot that I have ever read. As a naval aviator who flew two carrier combat tours in Vietnam and spent six years as a prisoner of war in Hanoi, I felt I was reliving my own life as I read Frank's diary entries. We who served in Vietnam all felt the same emotions—fear, elation, fatigue, strong camaraderie with our fellows, and, above all, frustration. As Frank expressed so well, we could not understand why we were not allowed to strike those targets and take those military actions that we knew were necessary to win the war; for example, mining Haiphong and destroying the rail link to China. Instead, we were required to conduct hazardous night bombing missions against truck convoys, the most inefficient means of interdicting logistics resupply to South Vietnam.

Frank flew in the most difficult phase of the air war in Vietnam. We had been conducting bombing missions over North Vietnam for almost two years in 1966, and our adversary had built up formidable air defenses, comprised of an intensive array of small arms, antiaircraft artillery, and radar-guided surface-to-air missiles (SAMS). We were the first aviators in history to fly against SAMS, and we learned early that our airplanes did not possess the electronic countermeasures capability to survive against this threat. We had to modify our airplanes quickly, as well as to develop new tactics for our bombing missions.

The administration was beginning to perceive at that time that our strategy of gradualism—what we called "squeeze them and wait"—was not working, and the president escalated the tempo and risk of our air operations. As Frank laments in his diary, our losses of planes and air crews were heavy in that period.

Frank Elkins embodied the finest qualities of the American national character. Our country must always produce persons such as he if we are to retain our greatness. And individuals such as Frank must always aspire to serve in our armed forces if we are to preserve our freedom and way of life in an often dangerous world.

As this book depicts, wars are grim and dirty affairs, seldom effective solutions to disputes between nations. We must continue to strive to develop the means of guaranteeing world peace and stability and always remember that the best way to prevent wars is to be well prepared to fight them.

—Vice Admiral William P. Lawrence, USN (Ret.)

Acknowledgments

I am grateful to the Elkins and Roberson families for their love; to my students for their acceptance; to Professors Wagner-Martin, Harris, Greene, Ludington, Harper, King, Eble, Stein, Sullivan, and Ramsey for their encouragement; to my graduate student friends for their support; and to Maggie and Kathy for their assistance.

Prologue

I had known that my husband was keeping a diary of his experiences as a pilot in Vietnam; he planned to write a novel after he returned and felt that a record of his own immediate reactions to the war would serve as valuable source material. I was not, however, prepared for the large volume that arrived shortly after October 12, 1966, when his name was entered on the list of men missing in action, eight months after our marriage.

With the diary I received a long letter from Barry Jones, an aviator friend of Frank's. Frank had selected Barry to act as his "censor" in the event Frank should be killed. Navy regulations required that the private papers of anyone killed or missing be read and any offensive material—such as profanity, a married man's letters from other women, or material of a classified nature—be removed before these papers are forwarded to the family. Barry's letter explained that he had not altered or deleted the text of Frank's diary. As a career military man, he was taking a risk by sending the unexpurgated diary to me, but he felt that he was taking a risk that Frank would have taken for him: "Reading Frank's diary I became upset by my own lack of sensitivity and have decided that I will not be responsible for changing one word of this diary." He added, "I think Frank is one of the most skillful and daring pilots I know. Until I read his diary, I never understood the cost of his apparent lack of fear."

A week later Barry was dead. He died in a fire which broke out on board the USS *Oriskany,* killing over thirty aviators. Barry's death freed me to publish the diary. But Frank was officially neither dead nor alive, and for almost six years I clung to the hope that he would return and use his diary as the basis of a novel.

In 1973, seven years after Frank's plane had been shot down, I decided to have his diary published. My daily visits to the North Vietnamese delegation in Paris, where I had been living for almost three years in an effort to obtain more information about Frank's status, had convinced me that he was dead. And I realized that the diary was too valuable to remain unpublished. Like Barry, I was frightened by the responsibility of editing such a personal account of someone else's life, but shortening the material and changing the names was imperative. My emotional response to this task seemed less important than the responsibility I felt to ensure that some tangible record of Frank's experience remain.

The diary met with moderate success, but the political climate at the time was not ripe for Vietnam commentary. That climate has changed, and it seems to me that the diary increases in importance. The public is now interested in the Vietnam war and the people who died there. Recent efforts to understand that experience more fully indicate that other Americans may still be seeking their own informed closure for the events of those traumatic years. I hope that this new edition of *The Heart of a Man* will help them in their healing process as well.

Knowing what others have felt and suffered assists any psychological recovery. The honesty of Frank's diary should be particularly helpful for those men who were engaged in aerial warfare in Vietnam, as well as for their families. Unlike the ground troops who were forced to choose between tangling with the Vietnamese or with the American military, naval pilots were free to turn in their wings at any time and thus eliminate their active participation in the war without fear of stockades, prisons, or court-martials. As a result, each pilot was forced to make almost daily decisions regarding his involvement in the war.

Why then did these men continue to fly? Did their physical distance from their victims separate them from their own humanity? Frank's diary offers at least part of the complex answer. It would be valuable simply for its detailed account of wartime life aboard an aircraft carrier, but it offers much more: a personal look at one man's struggle with the conflicting doubts and pressures of aerial warfare.

By adding my epilogue to this new edition, I hope I have also provided some insight into how a "presumed" death affects those who survive. In addition, I have tried to suggest how important the eventual recovery of a loved one's remains can be. I use the word "suggest" for I suspect that, like many who seek closure for the Vietnam war, I am just beginning to understand its significance.

—*Marilyn Elkins*

The Heart of a Man

May 27, 1966

Second day of the cruise, two days after my twenty-seventh birthday, I donned my green fatigues and pistol for the first time and flew a tanker hop. (Tankers are air-borne fuel standbys which permit other planes to refuel in the air.)

It was a nice day for flying—many low puffy clouds, but the clouds topped at 2400, and it was beautifully blue above. We're five hundred miles from San Diego and the nearest airfield. I'm eager to see the Pacific—I wish that we were going to the South Pacific rather than to war; I wish there were no war. I think we all wish that were true.

Danny said today that my acceptance papers are here for augmentation into the regular Navy. I'm hoping this will mean that I can get a full year's extension of sea duty. An extension would mean another cruise, and having never been shot at, I may be premature in asking for a lot before I taste a little. Still a year at sea, particularly flying combat missions, would guarantee me a better set of orders or serve as a better endorsement on any letter of request I originate.

June 6, 1966

Let me back up and write about Hawaii. We arrived about 9:00 Wednesday morning and were free to go ashore. I went in with Don, Ed, Richard, and Kerry, but I soon struck out on my own. I walked up a canyon through a long, beautiful hillside section of homes then across the University campus. I backtracked and rented a raring

½ mph speedster and more floated than drove around the salty canal by some of the nearby hotels. Then I walked to the Hilton Hawaiian Village, where the squadron gravitated all night.

The whole squadron was there about "half in the wind." When I arrived, the skipper and the commander of the air group (CAG) had already been asked to leave the club. Our mild-mannered skipper is the wildest man I ever saw on the beach. Not really bad, but throwing CAG's jock strap from table to table in the Hilton Garden Bar was fairly indicative of the weekend to come.

Thursday I flew one of those Christmas-Fourth-of-July-Kiss-from-your-favorite-girl-Trip-to-the-World-Series hops that every now and then fills you up to overflowing. We flew over Oahu, Pearl Harbor, the city, and down Waikiki Beach. Then to Molokai, where we found the leper colony. It was so lush and beautiful there that it was difficult to picture the diseased inhabitants. I had always imagined leper colonies as villages of huts with poor, sick people reduced to less than humans, but here was the colony bound on three sides by beautiful white shell beaches and on the fourth by a steep cliff overgrown with beautiful vines and brush. The cliff had a number of mountain-spring waterfalls running down its side.

Down on the island of Maui, I actually dipped my A-4 down inside the crater of Haleakala Volcano. Hawaii, the largest island, isn't very pretty, but there's a 13,000-foot mountain there which rises more sharply than the others and is fun to play near, just for the roller-coaster ride that the winds and turbulence give you.

During all our time in port, the skipper was promoting an annual palm-tree-climbing contest. He insisted that Johnny, last year's and now incumbent champion, was unbeatable. The contest is always held at a particular palm tree located directly in front of the Garden Bar so that the manager can call the police—the skipper's idea of a good time. Tim was bragging that he could beat anyone, and Barry took the bet. Tim went first and managed to climb some fifteen feet up that hard, sharp bark and was cut rather badly. Barry tied a rope between his feet the way the Polynesians do and was going great, hopping along the circular rounds of the tree. The string broke, and he continued with his bare hands and feet. He made sixty feet, higher than anyone had ever gone in past contests. When he climbed down, the sheriff had arrived and was ready to throw us all in the jug. The sheriff's big grumble was the great amount of wagering that had been going on among the tourists who had left their comfortable seats at the bar to watch the action. So Barry came down the new champion, and while the skipper assured the sheriff that he was a naval commander and not a bookie, we voted that Johnny had until 8:00 Sunday night to beat Barry's mark. I took one look at the terrible skins and cuts on Barry's arms and decided that I wanted no part of the whole affair.

Sunday morning I woke up with the miseries. I never felt so lonesome. It was just that everything was so beautiful that I needed to share it with Marilyn. I felt almost guilty that here was a world of beauty which I couldn't show her right then and there and, thereby, make it really my own.

I tried to shake it off, but finally, treat of the week, I called my favorite person in the world. We didn't get much said, but I felt warm and good for a little while. It made the lonelies and miseries have a keener edge a little later, though.

After I called Marilyn, the skipper made some asinine remark like "All that PT talk of yours is just for sissies; palm trees are men's play." So I made an ass of myself and climbed the tree, beating Barry's mark by ten feet. I climbed cold sober, cut my hands up, ruined my clothes, and gashed my left foot so badly that it needed a stitch or two. I gave it a bath in bourbon instead, and it hasn't turned blue yet.

June 12, 1966

Yesterday we were overflown by two Russian long-range bombers, known in Navy lingo as Bisons. Our F-8's (F8E Crusader Fighters) were launched, and the Bisons were intercepted about a hundred miles out from the ship and given an "escort" to and from the boat. Norris was launched in a duty-tanker to take pictures. Each aircraft—Russian and American alike—had all hands busy with cameras. The Russians were taking photos of the ship, the F-8's, the tanker, anything they could find. We did the same—a great cooperative effort on both sides, giving and obeying hand signals, positioning aircraft so that the other person could get a better picture. We have a picture of the Russian tail gunner, camera in hand, giving one of our F-8 pilots the international one-finger salute, the bird. I imagine the Russians have a similar picture of an F-8 driver. Norris landed the tanker and rushed down to Air Intelligence, saying that he had a great photo and wanted to get it developed right away. The picture came out a little overexposed, and there was an 18 × 20 shot of Norris's head with the Bison as a speck in the background! The photo is hanging in AI with the caption "An A-4 pilot watching a Russian Bison" and is the joke of the air group. [An A-4 is an A4C Skyhawk Attack Aircraft.]

Jack M., the Lt. Cdr. who was in survival school with me, was in-flight refueling behind Gerald and got some leakage from the buddy store down his intake, and his engine exploded and burned. He ejected, but had a lot of trouble getting into the copter. He got tangled in his parachute shroud lines while he was in the water and had to cut his way out of them. Made me stop and wonder what if this had happened over North Vietnam, where we'll be flying soon.

Today we're about seven hundred miles from Japan, maybe less. The seas have been pretty rough, and this tub rolls and pitches and slides down the troughs. We're not in a storm, but the feeling is the same. The very fact that we've been thousands of miles farther from land than I ever was in the Atlantic gives me an uneasy feeling. Jack M. mentioned this helpless feeling when he was in the water, a feeling of floating downward into that great limitless body. And the boat is tossed about on a seemingly calm ocean. And the wind is more than 40 knots across the deck today.

Barry and I finished off a pint of bourbon tonight and played darts. We talked until 02:00. Of all the air group, I like him best; he's intelligent and to-the-point; he's a formidable pilot who, in the air, shows brains and flair.

Funny, but my favorite pastimes shipboard are all tied up with Marilyn somehow: typing, playing the guitar, or playing darts. When I sit on the bed strummin' and hummin' with my eyes closed, my mind wanders through pleasant scenes like the brook across from her house. I dread getting to Japan. If I sit in port a few days without flying or working hard, it won't do my morale any good, and I know I must be putting her through the same paces.

June 14, 1966, Yokosuka, Japan

I'm daydreaming and thinking too much. A memory of a movie I once saw keeps coming back. It concerned a member of the elite fighting squadrons in the Japanese Air Force who was in on the bombing at Pearl Harbor and fought throughout the war. The thing that hit me was the way he looked at everything when the going was really good in the early stages of the war. Just like me, I mean; itching to get into things, absorbed in ribbons, medals, and glory, unlike old pros and unlike himself as he was later after involvement in the horror of losing.

It's not really like killing, somehow. You just roll in and drop bombs and see material things destroyed, but you don't hear the screams or see the splattering of blood and brains on walls and foliage or smoking metal. I imagine I'll have more to write and dream about that subject after I've actually seen some action. Yet I think it's something that I've always worried about.

I remember something Churchill said about war to the effect that nothing can compare with the turn which a young man's soul receives after being shot at in war and coming back alive. Shot at and missed, though, you understand. He didn't say a hell of a lot about the guy's soul who crashed in downtown Vinh, or the guy whose chute didn't open, or the one who drowned entangled in his shroud lines, or the pilot who bailed out over water, struggled to the feet-wet point, and was machine-gunned. Still, and I'm sure there's something to it, perhaps the guy who shot down the plane had a good turn done his soul. Well that's fine, but what a pity and a failure of human communication that our souls couldn't share this experience without such sacrifice. I'm not presuming to say that Churchill was wrong, for he knew and suffered all the horrors with which I am not even vaguely acquainted.

Today was the resolution of the stateroom scandal. All night long, Lt. Cdr.'s were poking their heads in staterooms, checking out the whole works, deciding what junior officers would be pushed out of choice spaces. Was I done in? Damn right. This wonderfully cool, air-conditioned, four-man room I'm in right now, down in the bowels of the ship, where just through the bulkhead I can hear the water rushing down the ship's hull as she plows along, this choice bit of real estate is mine only until tomorrow. One more night. Then instead of two Lt.'s and two Lt.jg.'s, it'll belong to three Lt. Cdr.'s. As for me, I'll be escaping Kurt's asinine remarks, but it's a nasty trick.

Good ole Norris. This morning at AI when we were bidding for rooms, Norris showed up in whites and wearing a pair of white shoes which had most of the toes chewed off (the work of his beagle, Norene). When his skipper asked him about it, he said, "Norene Lewis did it. She thinks about as much of the Navy as I do."

June 23, 1966
100 miles northwest of Okinawa

At last! Flight ops and a fast-pace day. The schedule kept me busy doing things for a change.

My new room is directly under the catapults, one deck down. Every time an AC (aircraft) goes—there goes another one—the whole room literally jumps. My glasses are all broken, and if you're in the rack, you are lifted up a little each time a plane goes off the ship.

Every night I make it a point to smoke at least two of the cigars which Marilyn's father sent me just to give myself some luxury to look forward to during the day. Strange the way you begin to look forward to small private pleasures like that.

Bob asked me yesterday how I got orders to VX-5, a test-pilot squadron, the best possible orders. How did I get orders? Hell, I didn't even know I had orders. I quickly made it up to admin., and there they were: orders to report to VX-5 in China Lake, California, in September of 66. Wahoo! Married life again. Everything will be perfect if I can just get through the next three months alive. Today the XO says my orders may be modified to extend me for the whole cruise. This will be exactly what I wanted before, but now I've been looking forward to being with HER. I wrote her yesterday, saying that I would be home in September. I

surely hate to write her about the possibility of my being extended, for it'll throw her into a sinking spell like nothing else can.

June 27, 1966, under way to Dixie Station off South Vietnam

Goddam boat! They're cycling the dadblamed catapults—your bones rattle and your ears ache with the loud, hollow echoing resonance.

I'm in the wardroom now because it's the only comfortable place on the whole goddam ship. I just left my hot-ass room because even the damned fan doesn't do anything for the humid heat beneath the cats. Shit, what a fat life! It's so hot that I sleep naked with no cover and still wake up soaking wet. I sweat so much that my mattress is wet; even my ankles sweat.

The shoals here are beautiful. The rock formation and shallow waters make a beautiful color from the air. It's funny; you get the impression you're over land there. Actually, you know you're still over water, but you feel safer around the shoals than you do out over the open sea. It's strange because the breakers would probably make short work of any survivor who parachuted into those treacherous waters.

On my second hop today, Bost and I were in the lead section with Don and Greg in second. We bombed the shoals and the wrecked ship, but this time we did so at night using MK-24 pyrotechnic flares to illuminate the target. From the very first, I was uneasy and uncomfortable, seeing the sun go down, knowing that I hadn't made a night landing on the carrier since the fourth of April—almost three months—and the weather was, in a word, shitty: low, blowing puffy stuff and black hairy lightning and thunderstorms in all quadrants. The bombing went okay though, and I forgot my uneasiness till we were off target and en route back to the ship. Then I started dreading making the landing on the ship—plus the added attraction of flying Don Bost's wing, which is always a thrill at night. He pumps the stick like he is drawing water. Even the wings of his plane seem to have a nervous twitch.

He finally left me at marshall near another storm at 140°, 44 nm from the ship at 29M, with a good, strong, serious case of 30°-left-wing-down-equals-vertigo. I fought and fought that sensation for four or five minutes. Finally my balance started believing the instruments, and I got the vertigo under control. I put my hook down and commenced my letdown at 20:19, set the power, and checked and rechecked for things I might have forgotten. Radar picked me up at twenty miles and brought me in. I've never had such a sensation of being able to think so much so fast as when I was on the ball, in close, just prior to landing. Things were buzzing through my head like lightning: "Kid, if you bolter after fighting that vertigo, you need your tail kicked—easy don't be rough with the power pole." I got aboard, settling to the ramp to a number-one wire—piss-poor driving—but I smiled when I felt the tug of the gear and really wanted to holler, "MADE IT"—cheated death again.

I decided that maybe I'm cool enough to go to my tiny-ass room, so I climb the ladders, cross the goddam hurdles, rearrange things in the room, get out my typewriter, and reach for this sheet, and the sonofabitchin electricity goes out again. Such a miserable existence—and I have a far better lot than most, being a Lt.

And today we're really off to war. I feel as unprepared as I have ever been. Four days from now we'll be dropping bombs on people; that's difficult to believe. I don't know how I'll feel about it; I hate to even wonder because taking someone's life and then wondering how *you* feel about it is harsh, to say the least.

We'll be flying close air support for ground operations for about a week. This is quite safe, actually, since South Vietnam has no great antiaircraft system of guns. It's sort of a transition phase, leading up to the more dangerous North Vietnam work. I'm glad, since I'm still not used to the idea.

What a damn hot-ass boat! Sweat in bed, sweat in your chair, I even sweat in the shower!

Well, the damned cats are shaking the whole room again. Goddam boat!

June 30, 1966, Dixie Station

Today was our first day of actual combat flying. I almost gagged in my mask when the forward air controller (FAC) said they were shooting at us. The FAC's are Air Force men who fly down fairly low in light Piper Cub-type aircraft and control all close air support in South Vietnam, except that done by B-52's. The shots being fired at us were small-arms fire, and nobody was hit all day.

I had only one hop. We were to hit a barracks area, under the control of a FAC, about forty-five miles north-west of Saigon. When we arrived, there was a goodly battle going between U.S. Cavalry troops and the VC. Darell had a big 1700# bullpup air-to-ground missile and four 500#

bombs. Glenn and I had two small bullpups (480#) and four 250 pounders. Joe was along in Bob's place on my wing and had a couple of napalm fire bombs and some 250#. We dropped them all on the jungle area across the road from our guys, shooting each time for an area marked off by the FAC with hand smoke grenades or rockets with smoke/flare heads. The FAC shot these where he wanted us to drop our bombs. Compared to the lot of these men who serve as FAC's—flying all day right over the enemy, vulnerable to small-arms fire, living near the scene on small dirt-strip camps which are regularly raided and mortared—this shipboard stuff is a gentleman's war.

Of course, it's like riding a motorcycle; you don't have any minor accidents. You hardly ever get hurt just a little bit. Yet I would hate to be an Army type down there, thrashing around in the bamboo and vines and snakes at 120 degrees in thick uniforms with heavy gear to lug through the woods—not to mention the humidity in a tropical rain forest.

South Vietnam is beautiful. From the air it looks a lot like Florida, all green and swampy. It's as easy for me to imagine that I'll soon be seeing Gainesville, Florida, as it is for me to picture the dying which must be occurring on that beautiful countryside. There is a redness of the soil that shows even through the foliage, and from the air, this red soil is the only striking difference from Florida.

One of our mission flights will be to set the VC rice fields on fire (we hear that they are short on food for the first time). These operations are appropriately called "Rice Krispie" missions. Cute, eh?

I've been reading too many war novels. I deeply believe in what's happening here, and I don't for a moment think it's not necessary. Still war is legal murder, and dropping bombs is a convenient impersonal way to be engaged. The war on the ground presents additional problems. Men are maimed and hardened and wounded merely by the sight of their own destructive powers, and although I know I'm doing something necessary and striking a blow for the things I'm pledged to defend, I don't like to think what really happens when the bombs land, or worse, what the area looks like after we drop our bombs and leave. I don't want to think that we are committing a modernized form of carnage and ruthless slaughter, covering the ground with bloody bodies and misshapen men.

July 1, 1966, Dixie Station

This morning the damned air conditioner was off, and I awoke at dawn sweating like hell. As Joe says, "Lawd, if it gits any hotter I'm gonna melt just like a big popsicle on a stick!" Hot and humid.

Two flights for the kid today. On the first flight, Glenn, my wingman, was sloppy and crappy looking. Bob is an ideal wingman; Glenn could be, but he just doesn't give a damn. He doesn't take criticism well either, takes everything personally and sulks and fails to improve in the air. I had another acquaintance like that who wound up in a charred, burnt-black, plowed-out furrow of woods six miles south of Cecil Field in Jacksonville, and it doesn't bother me one iota to jump all over Glenn with both feet. If he's sulking, that means that he's still alive. If he busts his ass now, it'll be because he did it in spite of advice and no fault of mine. Bob Smith's formation is great! On the way back from the strike, Bob joined up close, and I gave him the free cruise signal. Then as Darell and Glenn led back, I took Bob through barrel rolls and wingovers.

After that first flight, dropping all our ordnance in 45° dives on a portion of jungle said by the FAC to be a VC headquarters, I felt I had done a day's work, and it was only 09:30.

The second hop was tremendous. We were to bomb a Viet Cong billeting area north of Than something-or-other, thirty miles inland, but we were diverted and sent to bomb a cluster of buildings fifteen miles south of Saigon. We dropped our heavy stuff first and then made drops with the lighter bombs. I made the grand finale by sweeping in low from the opposite direction from the previous runs and dropping one napalm, on each of two runs, on the buildings, setting them on fire. The first bomb was a good hit, and one end of the tin-roof building was ablaze. The second barely missed the top of the building, but with fire bombs an inch miss is damned near good as a mile. FAC said we completely destroyed two of the concrete buildings and severely damaged the other two.

One of the most impressive things about the area where we rendezvoused with the FAC in his L-19 was the mile-after-mile area of solid lines of craters, undisputedly the work of the Air Force B-52's. You would see a crater, then a space about twice the width of a crater, then another crater, and the line would continue in that pattern for miles. Parallel to that line and close by, there was another line—like rows of corn, or trees in an orchard. They really must have done some careful planning, for friendly villages were fairly close at hand. We had been warned that we must be particularly accurate today, for we were operating very close to a friendly village.

My flying was okay; I'm getting the old knack back. If I only had some talent to go with this love of the air and of the machine, I'd have it made. Let's just hope that I am as enthusiastic after my second day up north.

It never occurs to you while you're flying that there are people down there. Barry and I talked about this tonight. The area we hit yesterday was walked through afterward by the cavalry units, and the body count of VC was up around six hundred. Both Barry and I admitted that we feel ashamed that the bombing and shooting doesn't really affect us deeply. The real shame that I feel is my own lack of emotional reaction. I keep reacting as though I were simply watching a movie of the whole thing. I still don't feel that I have personally killed anyone. Somehow the whole experience remains unreal. Have I become so insensitive that I have to see the torn limbs, the bloody ground, the stinking holes and guts in the mud, before I feel ashamed that I have destroyed numbers of my own kind? The bombing is right, I think, but who am I? Humans have always decided what is right, and these same humans have sometimes decided later that they may have been wrong. I only hope and pray that I don't change my mind about what I am doing here. I will lose my mind if I do.

Another letter from Marilyn today. She does write good letters. I couldn't have chosen a better life's companion, not anywhere, no better complementary personality, no more outspoken conscience for me.

July 2, 1966
Dixie Station

I'm still worrying about those "six hundred dead." Possibly the count is an exaggeration. I won't feel bad, I don't think, as long as I can think of the target as a group of buildings or a supply dump, or a petrol storage area—as long as I can avoid seeing the whites of their eyes, and more important, as long as I can believe that those I do kill, I kill quickly and, to that extent, painlessly.

Tonight I saw *Cleopatra* in the wardroom. It's like a night out; you get a shower and put on some good stinkum, dress in some freshly starched khakis, and go "out" to a movie.

I'm really pleased that I'll be going to China Lake in September. That means Marilyn will have to wait awhile before starting work on her master's, but she sounds even more excited than I am—I just hope the whimsical Navy makes no more changes in my orders. I would prefer to complete this cruise, but only if I could be certain of getting a second set of orders as a test pilot. That ain't likely if I'm forced to stay on this tub past September. These orders are the cat's cream.

July 3, 1966
Dixie Station

It's after midnight now and the end of my fourth day on Dixie Station.

On my second flight, the FAC led us to a wooded area, where we orbited a few minutes till some low clouds blew by. Then he marked an area of woods south of the river using a smoke rocket. Again we bombed without actual visual contact with the enemy. Then the fun part of the day began. We agreed to meet the spads, single-engine, propeller-driven planes from the A-D squadron of the ship, at 040°, 30 nm, 10M for a big twilight dogfight. (One of the spad's main functions is to fly protective cover for helicopter rescues of downed pilots.) It was dark by the time we rendezvoused. Radios sounded something like this:

"Hey, I'm rolling in at 160° on a low speed."

"Okay, is that you above me? Flash your lights."

"Holy hell, who just went by me?"

"Was that you? I thought you were the spad. Chip, do you hold us?"

"I think so; flash your beacon—hey, look out, they've got a sleeper up high—Who's that above me?"

"Goddam, I just met him head-on. I thought he was going the other way."

And so it went. If you think 150 knots in the tip of a high yo-yo with 120° bank and 1.5 G's is a hairy trick in the daytime, try it in the black of night with three A-D's and three A-4's and a sky filled with stars that look like aircraft lights until you try to rendezvous with them and stall and fall. Whee, but it was fun—Chip came back white!

Everyone seems to consider me the pilot that I feel I am. I've raised pure hell in almost every flight I've flown and impressed most of the people with whom I've flown. If there were a who-is-the-best-pilot-in-the-squadron contest, I think that I would win. I have to continue to prove myself to myself, but as long as I succeed, I guess I'm okay.

I'm mighty undecided about leaving in September. I want to see Marilyn and do all the things we could do, but I would also like to get all the air medals, etc., and more particularly I feel that I need the combat experience. Of course, I am speaking without having flown against enemy fighters, enemy AAA, and enemy SAM's. As George Johnson used to say, "Those that want to go are those that ain't been." Now I fall into that group. Still . . . I am undecided. The real advantage I'd like to gain is that extra year of seniority that I would have on my contemporaries by "dragging my feet" and getting an extra year of sea duty. If I stay on sea duty for another year, I'll be rotating along with people a year my junior, and I'll always have that one-year jump on them as far as seniority in billet choices. I want to give the whole thing some more thought after I've seen the flying steel and lead. Then I think I'll know.

I must have made friends with Tim. He just brought me a cold San Miguel Filipino beer which, aboard ship, is worth at least a small fortune. I have a fifth of bourbon and gin, but beer is bulky and, therefore, logistically impractical—and all the more wonderful a surprise.

Independence Day, Dixie Station

Turns out that Richard is the one really funny guy in our outfit, and he is game for anything—dogfight to poker game. He's always making some false, raving charge against someone. Today he tore into me for getting so much mail from Marilyn. He's really good company, and we played gin a lot until we hit the combat zone. It's been nothing but max thrust since we arrived.

Joe's been in on a couple of hops on which BDA (bomb damage assessment) gave him credit for several people's death. And, like me, it's a different case when you know that you've killed for sure 'cause now you've got to be right in what you're doing. Killing reaches way inside you and searches for the truth. I see Joe feeling this now. We both believe in what we're doing, but still there's something to face every time it happens.

This morning I led Bob and Ralph across the country over to the Cambodian border, where there had been a major battle yesterday between the Charlies and the U.S. Infantry. The VC were in retreat and were in a wooded area near a friendly rubber plantation. We each had eight 250# bombs, and we pounded the wooded area with our ordnance. It seemed just like flying down to Stevens Lake and "bombing" for a while.

What a big zero Bost is! Tonight I really went out with the tigers: Bost-Toastie, Ralphie, and Jerry. What an enthusiastic challenging hop! I lost my oxygen at the start of the flight, and when I mentioned it on our way back to the ship, I thought Bost would spin in. Ralph lost his radio, and Bost loused up bringing him aboard so badly that when they landed they had messages to see both the CAG and the captain right away. Bost is the third officer in command. What a sterling example for the rest of us to live up to!

For me flying is just pure fun—danger or not—and I can see how some people consider Navy pilots as members of a refined motorcycle club. Damn, though, I love to fly. I zoomed up a vertical cloud today and in my heart the words of Gillespie's "High Flight" came welling: "Oh I have slipped the surly bonds of earth/ and danced the sky on laughter silvered wings."

I spent some time today reading and rereading Marilyn's letters. She's it as far as the kid is concerned. There can't be but one, and I decided six months ago that for the rest of my life, however long that might be, she's the one. If I've ever made a decision that paid me back in the deep hours of the lonely night, this was it. In my life I've loved three entities that deserved it: my mother, because she unselfishly wanted only what I wanted for me; my flying, because it gave me joy and self-respect; and Marilyn, because I've never felt so close to another human being. Her letter describing the kittens and rain displays just the sort of feeling and sensitive understanding which so endears her to me. She says that she bungles, but what she manages to do is hit the very heart of things I know that I've felt only after she tells me about them.

July 8, 1966

What a hot SOB this whole tub is! Outside my door in the passageway, the thermometer says 94 degrees, and it's 10:00 at night. At noon today it was 105 degrees here in this room. I'd ten times rather be on a combat mission in my nicely air-conditioned cockpit with people shooting at me than supposedly getting a day of rest on this furnace.

One of the things the Air Force does occasionally is to spray wide stretches of jungle with defoliates which kill the leaves and vines and rob the Viet Cong of their hiding places. When we were flying in the south, we flew over one of these areas and dropped fire bombs on it to set it on fire and maybe smoke out some of the VC. Well, the air is so wet and volatile that when the heat from the fire started rising above the fire, it caused a small thunderstorm right over itself and put the fire out within fifteen minutes. At first we didn't know what was happening, but when we tried it again the next day, it happened again; the heat caused the air to rise and form rain clouds. That's the best example I know of how wet and humid it is in this country. Add that humidity to the steam of the cats, and it's no wonder that all I do is bitch about the heat.

It was our first day to fly over the north, and I was handed a tanker hop so I still don't know what the big action is like. Don and Richard went out on the same launch as my tanker and destroyed nine river barges they happened to find.

The staff captain in the War Room explained how the North Vietnamese continue to supply their troops in the south. Three main routes the NVN use are all almost directly parallel and within twenty-five miles of each other and run practically the length of North Vietnam. These routes are the railroad, the main highway itself (the one we call "Highway 1-A"), and the coastline waterway. Supply troops carry something by bicycle for a distance, then transfer it to the railroad and run it perhaps thirty miles by rail, then transport it to the road if a railroad bridge is out, or put it on a barge. You can't blow up rivers, and we sink barge after barge and still they come. All this river traffic—junks, barges, flatboats, etc.—are cheaply made, so there's no real problem to replace them. To that extent it's a game of patience; who'll get tired of the war first, a test of endurance.

July 9, 1966

There was a special meeting in the ready room at 09:00 this morning. All aviators were forced to get up to attend the meeting. The purpose of the meeting? The skipper wanted to warn us not to get complacent. Can you get that? We fly until after midnight, and the skipper routs everyone out of bed to tell us not to get complacent. How about getting rested, skipper, how about that, how about a little sleep on this hot-ass boat where twelve hours of sleep equals eight because of the goddam heat!

At 11:15 I briefed for my first "combat" hop over North Vietnam. What an abortion! The skipper (to whom Heaven would be a thirty-plane echelon with himself in the lead going in parade formation into Hanoi) led the flight with Chip on his wing; Joe and I were in the second section. We approached the beach. We were supposed to make our run from the south, down Highway 1, dropping one instantaneous and three chemical delay fused ANM 64 (500# GP's) on a little piddly-ass bridge north of Vinh. Approaching from the southeast, do we make our run from the south, up the road? No, we fly over the target (waking everybody up so they can get a chance to fire at us), then do a 270° turn to the left. If anybody in town had been awake with a gun, some of us would not have come back.

Tonight I go out with Darell on a night armed reconnaissance hop. Bost-Toastie spares the flight, and if he gets to go, I'd almost not go—except that I like to consider myself somewhat daring—and to go anywhere with that zero is to just dare death. What a complete ineffective!

Combat jitters are not too noticeable about the ship except in isolated cases. The XO of one squadron turned in his wings on July 6, having had enough. He was to be sent off on the COD (Carrier-on-deck-delivery, an S2-F) and flown to Cubi Point in the Philippines. When you are a passenger in a COD, you are strapped in your seat backward for the catapult shot. When he was catted off, his straps came loose, and he pitched forward and smashed his head into the bulkhead. He cut his head from the back of his scalp across his head and all the way down the right side of his face. They brought the COD around and landed again, and he has been in the operating room for hours now. He had quit because he had premonitions of a forthcoming crash. Louie had the watch, saw the whole thing, and said, "When I turn in my wings, I want to go ashore in a long boat."

July 10, 1966

Nobody can say that my first night hop wasn't exciting, though I never saw a bullet. First of all there was the year's blackest catapult shot. It was still so hot on deck at 22:45 that the sweat ran down in my eyes and blinded me as the cat fired me off the ship. Once airborne and rendezvoused, we headed 265° for our coast-in-point. Nearing the beach, we went to air-to-air tacan, turned our lights out, and I took two miles separation aft of Darell and 1000 feet above him. We found the target area—the road/canal network alongside Ha Tinh (checkpoint 24), a moderate flak site. Darell went in at 4M, heading south from the 1230 peak where we "feet-dried." He dropped his first flare, a dud. That set the pace for the remainder of the evening. The rest of the night was one *faux pas* after another.

First of all, I noticed that I had not turned on my ALQ-51 missile and fire-control radar warning/countermeasure. When you turn that device on, the standby light burns until the set warms up, then goes out. Well, it was black as Mooney's goose anyway, but when the standby yellow light came on it just blinded me. First minute of nighttime over enemy territory, and I'm blinded by my own stupidity in not turning the thing on earlier.

So, Darell's first flare was a dud. By this time I had lost my tacan, and we were coordinating the section by radio only. He called turning left, and I had no idea where he was, but I climbed to a perch hoping his second flare would give me a target and get us together again—another dud flare.

This time I went in to drop a flare, not knowing where I was. I told Darell that I would drop a flare and he could tell me where to put a second flare in relation to the first. But my first flare was right over a large waterway, and Darell sighted barges below and called rolling in. On my first run, when I depressed the bomb-release button, my altitude gyro quit, the instrument lights went dim, and it looked like my electrical power was failing. I still had my peanut (standby) gyro, though, so I said the hell with it, I'll drop my bombs. The flare went out, so I made a turn to the left toward the beach and came in heading south again.

It takes a little mental discipline to make oneself fly at 4000-foot level and 250 knots to release the flares at optimum conditions. I dropped the second flare too far east and didn't light any decent target. By this time I had begun to get what sounded like fire-control radar "singing" in my earphones, and I was pretty wary of the whole affair. My electrical system was still playing wild games. I dropped a dud flare and had to set up to drop my last one—Darell's had all been duds. My last flare turned up a bridge with truck traffic crossing it, and we headed in for it. I set up a 30° dive, planning for a 4000-foot release of all my bombs, but again I forgot my right-wing station select switch and wound up dropping only my two 500# MK-82's off my left wing. So there I was with no gyro, no tacan, a failing electrical system, and a 1000# asymmetrical load, and before I could get back around the circle, the flare went out.

I let my eyes adapt a moment, though, and thumbnailed the bridge and made a full-black, shoot-from-the-hip run on it—and blew it out of the water!

I joined back up with Dan off the beach. My air conditioner had also been hard to control. When I secured my armament switches, I got my gyro back, but it would not erect. Once we had joined up and settled down, Darell told me to try the emergency generator. I tried this and it worked okay, but it didn't solve any problems. Still no gyro. So we agreed to stay together and see if the gyro erected. It never did, and I rode his wing down to landing with the following complications: my canopy began to freeze over, and I couldn't see shit; Darell had no external lights so I was forced to fly formation on two feet of his wingtip instead of a whole airplane. We leveled off, and I manually overrode the air conditioner, by-passed the emergency generator, and defrosted the canopy. Then we had to dive to get down to approach altitude, working like a mother all the while.

To top off the hop, at fifteen miles, the air conditioner went to full hot and just about ran me out of the plane. By the time I landed, I was sopping, soaking wet and weak as hell.

I am now standing the duty officer watch. Pilots have just manned their aircraft for the first flight of the day. The skipper is leading a sort of baby Alpha strike against a railroad yard at Qui Minh. He'll lead a four-plane group in from the east while another strike swings in from the south and hits a by-pass construction area three miles away. We have a two-plane "Ironhand" or flak suppression flight orbiting off the beach armed with two antiradiation missles. If radar sites are sighted, then shrikes are lobbed in, and they home in on the radar transmissions and knock out the radar.

I still can't say anything about how I react to flak and gunfire. It's funny—I don't want to be shot, and the best way to avoid it is to avoid being *shot at,* but with everyone dodging bullets and coming back a little shaken, I'm anxious to know how it will affect me. Of course, I'm sure that if affects one in different ways depending upon multiple reasons ranging from your wife's last letter to what you had for breakfast. In that regard, I'm safe. Still I may be unconsciously afraid.

After last night's hop, perhaps more because I was tired, I dreamt all night of being in an aircraft in which I couldn't see anything. It was more terrible for being a dream. The terror was in struggling for awareness—I couldn't tell what the aircraft was doing—like struggling to see something, or more nearly like struggling to stay awake when you're sleepy and driving and know that you must stay awake.

It was a stupid dream, but it started from the hop, of course. I wonder what sort of dreams I'll have a month from now?

An F-8 showed get-aboard-itis last night and dived for the deck, collapsing his port wheel and setting himself and the flight deck afire. He got out okay, but in the rush to the scene a chief petty officer ordnanceman was pushed into a knee-knocker and trampled. He had a big half-moon cut across his head above his forehead—fourteen internal stitches and twenty-six along the cut. Cdr. Smith is still in the hospital. His injury on the COD left him with a fractured skull, broken jaw, and uncounted stitches; they sewed on him for some three hours. Bad news. And the count begins.

I hope the professional nature of the war yields results along the lines of steady nerves. For, as Barry says, there's rarely been a war such as this when men could say, "I've had enough," and be sent home the next day. For those of us in the Naval air war in Vietnam, it's a volunteer war. And to that extent, it's a professional war. At the same time, it would be extremely difficult to turn in your wings and quit, even if you were afraid for your life, in the company of those with whom you've never been a quitter before.

Back to the action at hand. The skipper's flight just returned. All bombs were delivered with good results on the railroad yard, and the other flight knocked out the pile driver on the construction site, a bridge, and scored a direct hit on a flak site with secondary explosions galore. Everybody's happy!

July 11, 1966

I'm a little shaken tonight, but not much; just the sight of muzzle flashes from the automatic stuff on the ground. Haven't been near any big stuff yet, but I'll go tomorrow on an Alpha strike on the Haiphong petroleum storage area. I'm not worried so much about being shot at as I am about worrying. If I don't worry, I'm fat; if I don't get the shakes and mess up, I'm okay, except, of course, for the element of chance.

Tonight I blew a bridge out on one of the main highways and destroyed about six barges; at least I'm convinced they were barges. I could work myself into an emotional problem if I let my mind wander into the possibility that they might have been family fishing junks. But they were flat and covered with canvas and out on one of the main canals and appeared to be hauling freight. I'm glad that most people I talk to feel the same as I do about that, any but military targets are taboo. Cdr. White didn't feel that way; I don't think he minded just lofting a bomb into a village any more than he minded dropping a practice bomb on a fake target. I'm sure that we can all mind too much for our emotional health, but I ache when I think of love stories of peasant people, stories of old men and women who but for time and luck would have no part in the dispute for power, when I think of my own life and its twists and turns—and the interruption, sudden and final, that I may be making to make some hapless mistake—a barge? A legitimate military target, hauling aid and supplies to the enemies of what we believe? Or a poor family's home and means of livelihood? I can say again and again that those were military targets, but down deep inside I have to pray that I did right.

We went out on this flight at sunset. We found traffic and light enough to bomb without flares. I had planned to make a run to the west and pull off south, but I saw automatic gunfire popping at us from the south and turned north, and there was the bridge in an opportune place. So I bagged it, first time.

As I was pulling off the bridge, my surface-to-air missile (SAM) warning light began flashing. I remember as I called, "SAM's away," not having any fear or funny sensation running through me. I only realized that I was frightened later when I discovered that I was alive and safe. I remember looking at my hands—as if they were the whole of me and their being intact signified no damage done. Bost was calm. Amazing. And great! I don't dislike him; I just hate his mediocre handling of his job.

Turned out it wasn't a SAM at all, just some strange lights. So here I sit raving about SAM's, and I've never seen

33

one coming at me. Nothing but muzzle flashes of automatic guns, and a few radar warnings of fire-control radar tracking me. I wonder how I'll feel tomorrow night; there are twenty-five to thirty SAM sites surrounding Haiphong, each capable of firing six missiles. And flak and automatic gunfire thick as leaves on an elm. I think tomorrow night I will have found out what I came out here to know. I somehow feel that tomorrow night I'll know all about a Navy career, will have toyed with the essence of the whole business. And I don't know how I'll feel.

July 12, 1966

It's 22:00, 12 July 66, and I'm damned glad to be alive! We hit the oil storage area between Haiphong and Hanoi this morning, and the excitement was a little strong for my taste. Lemme tell ya, I'm paying back in full for all those fun hops around Cecil Field in Jacksonville, for trips to the Caribbean, for Christmas in Rome; all paid in full as of 12:30 today. Actually paid in full as of 11:45, when I saw the black puffs of explosive shells after my butt, mine because I was the only one in the area. I guess that's what I came for, to pay for my good life.

Here's how it went. I volunteered to go. I lost my gyro and compass on deck but went anyway. I was CAG's wingman. I made my run on the target and lost sight of CAG. I had no compass but thought that I knew my way out and

ran—full bore for ten minutes—longest in my life except for those fifteen minutes I spent in that black box at survival school.

An F-8 was shot down. We were twenty miles from the Chinese border. The radio sounded like this:

"Hey Paul, are you in 'burner'?"

"Negative."

"Then you're on fire. Now there're flames all over your bird! Get out!"

"Negative."

"You're going to explode. Eject! Eject!"

"Negs."

Then the CAG came on the radio. "Better get out of it, Bud, no chance!"

Then the pilot, a Lt.jg. I didn't know, cool as ice says, "Well, sorry about that . . . see ya next year!" and punched out.

He was on the ground for an hour and a half. A chopper picked him up with spads and F-8's flying cover. When he got back, his squadron met him en masse on the flight deck. He kissed the deck, posed for pictures, did a dance, and rode shoulders to the ready room.

Donald, the flight surgeon, had a shot of bourbon waiting for all of us.

A photo plane flew over the oil site and found that three out of four of the big oil tanks were destroyed, a beautiful success. The BDA was 75 per cent destruction, better than we hoped.

Our best protection from SAM's lies in the fact that at China's demand Russia pulled her technicians out, and the Chinese and Vietnamese don't know how to maintain and operate the gear most effectively. We also have anti-radar missiles which home on the SAM's guidance radar and occasionally score a hit. I commit my own butt, however, to an aircraft control stick which never stays still, turning, diving, climbing, "jinking," anytime I'm over land, making myself a hard computer problem for a fire-control radar operator.

They're building a big gun site on the coast, big enough to fire at our destroyers and smaller craft in the water. We'll probably wait until they've done a lot more work on it and spent a lot more money, then strike it before the guns are mounted.

I hope Marilyn realizes that the USN is a whimsical animal and that my orders can be changed. I keep worrying about that message about all pilots making all the cruise with no midcruise transfers. With my orders to VX-5 in my hand, I'm hoping that's just a policy guide for future planning, but one never knows.

The XO says that the skipper will make the final decision about my orders. I told the skipper that I wanted to make a whole combat cruise, but when I received my orders and saw that they were for VX-5, I decided that these orders were too good to pass up for two extra months on the line. Since I don't know what the final decision will be, I can't tell Marilyn what to expect, and I'm rather confused about what I really want to do.

July 14, 1966

Days are really messed up now. We're flying from midnight to noon, and sleeping has to come in the afternoon or catch-as-catch-can at night.

Last night Bob and I had the first go. I led him on the Route 1-A from Ha Tinh to Vinh. I was sleepy when we launched, and it was dark as pitch. It was so black that even with instrument lights turned max low, I couldn't distinguish land from sea from 15,000 feet. So, we turned out all our lights and stumbled around, descending to 5000 feet, and found the coast. I had planned the same flare drop points as I used before, and my first went right over the highway, but we didn't see any traffic. So we regrouped over the coast, dodged a couple of light AAA sites that were firing on us there, and went in on a different heading/timing run. This time we didn't see anything at first. Then I spotted a bridge standing over a wide canal which would really hurt road traffic and rolled in on it. As I was rolling in, Bob saw some traffic on the road near the bridge, so we had some luck. My hits were off, at first, and I missed the bridge by 100 feet, but my miss was better than a hit, for we got three secondary explosions which had to be either hidden vehicles of a petroleum or arms storage area. We then got some resistance, tracers coming from the north at a pretty thick rate, more at Bob than at me. We dropped all our bombs there and came back to the ship about 01:30.

The *Constellation* hit a railroad/highway bridge near Nam Dinh not too long ago and had a lot of resistance from MIG's. So our fighters, hot for a hassle, flew the same route hoping to stir up the MIG's and have at them. It backfired. The MIG's came all right, but they shot the hell out of us. I wasn't on the hop, but it was a fouled-up affair. There were F-8's yelling "Break right, there's another one of them on your six," "Reverse, reverse!" Cdr. Bowden got shot up, overstressed what was left of his aircraft, couldn't inflight refuel, and ran out of fuel twenty-five miles short of the Da Nang divert field. He ejected over water and is okay. That's four F-8's we've lost in four days, and all of them from the same squadron. No pilots lost yet, though.

During the last year the Navy has dropped tons and tons of ordnance on the Thanh Hoa highway bridge, and it just keeps standing. Well, last night, or rather this morning at 00:50, Merve was programmed to hit a highway bridge south of Thanh Hoa. He got lost and wandered into Thanh Hoa, the worst flak area outside of Vinh and Hanoi/Haiphong, saw a bridge, bombed it, and knocked out the formidable Thanh Hoa bridge. He'll probably get a DFC (Distinguished Flying Cross) for it. And partly for getting lost. Hell, half the successes out here are accidents. I probably got my best hit last night by missing the target for which I aimed.

July 15, 1966

Actually it's July 16 at 00:50 hours. I have a brief in one and a half hours, and I can't sleep. I had a dream a week or so ago that Marilyn gave me my rings back for some reason, just handed them to me without a word, and I haven't had a letter from her in three days. That's not long, but longer than normal. I remember how on the night Carl and Bill were killed, I woke up from a sound sleep and said, "Carl's dead." Then I said, "Oh, crap," and went back to sleep until Marilyn called me to give me the news. I keep remembering that tonight and thinking about Marilyn and letting my mind run wild like she probably does sometimes too. That's part of the difficulty; the fact that she can be imagining as much there as I am here.

I'm also worried about the Alpha strike tomorrow. Bob and I are to fly Ironhand flak/SAM suppression in support of the strike on one of the road/railroad bridges south of Hanoi, carrying six MK-82's each, a hell of a load to be dragging around way the hell inland. I'm more hesitant than I had expected to be, though I keep expecting to get better. This morning I was cool and calm when Bob and I struck the bridge at Qui Vinh, and that was worst of all. It was the first time since the Alpha strike on the oil depot near Hanoi/Haiphong that I had flown a daylight hop, and both my big AGM 126 bullpup missiles went wild as hell and hit off in the middle of nowhere. I was completely cool and calm, and the missiles went crazy. I felt that this was the most futile attempt of all. My hits on the Alpha strike were long and landed in the water. I might as well have stayed home. I seem to get through my strikes at night on pure guts, sweat, tears, and raw chance, and I don't think I've even scared a soul but myself yet. I'm sure rationally that I have, but I can't make myself feel I've been good enough.

Feeling this way gets people killed too, thinking you've got to do well today to make up for lesser hops, pressing too hard, too low, too long, and being blown out of the sky. I'm fighting this already. I'm just damned determined to hit something useful, to bust up something that'll really hurt, and to do it tonight.

But that Alpha strike tomorrow. As Barry Jones and Jerry say, "My courage diminishes in proportion to the distance inland," and this route takes us right into the heartland where all the SAM's, MIG's, flak, AAA, and population are. High chance of being hit, high chance of hitting civilians, no chance of evasion if you are shot down. And my job is to put down any resistance from the deck with bombs, which means no standoff distance. If some-body starts shooting or firing SAM's, I look down his gun barrel, run head on, and bomb him. Some excitement, eh journal?

Early this morning (01:45–03:40), Chip and I had a coastal armed reconnaissance hop. We flew in and rendez-voused north of Qui Vinh; from there we flew fifteen miles north. On my first flare run, nothing. On my way in for the second, I noticed lights from a convoy on the deck and instead of rolling in on it in the dark, I dropped a flare and didn't see them. We had good hits on the road and railroad, but you can never tell whether you're really hurting the Charlies or if they're just down there laughing at you and hauling the garbage south despite all we can do.

I can see how the Korean War U.S. pilots could become obsessed with the idea of knocking down those doggoned bridges. I'm gonna get me a bridge tonight!

I read in the Air Intelligence Office tonight of Cdr. Midford's "confession" about the war—how his "heart hadn't been in it." I remember him as a real tiger. I find the "confession" to be something of a fiction, except that I could surely regret personal involvement if I were in a prison camp or interrogated daily and brainwashed. But that's like regretting a poker game after you lost, you can't say that you didn't know the chances before you started. The F-8 pilot shot down on the Alpha strike said he heard loudspeakers in the nearby villages calling out, probably, he figured, to tell the local citizens to capture the enemy pilot. Pilots are quite valuable alive, more so than dead, and these confessions are one of the reasons why.

I notice that I am very easily irritated and very impatient with little things people do or say. It's partly the long hours, partly disappointment in my first few flights, and to a large degree it is in reaction to other pilots' irritability. I don't like being kidded about anything. Bill's been rubbing me wrong today. I try to pay him no mind, but I'm chafed a little by any teasing. I wish that Barry and I were in the same section.

It's 01:30. Flight operations just sounded. I'm lying here naked in bed with the air vent open and a fan blowing on me, leaving a damp outline of myself on the sheet and pillow beneath me, and brushing sweat from my eyebrows and temples. Lord keep me in this discomfort, though, and out of the hell of North Vietnam terra firma.

I need a letter from Marilyn. I know that she has written—she writes me every day—it's just a lapse in delivery, but I'll feel better when I have her letters in my hand. I didn't write her today. I should, but I just felt too bad about the bullpup hop to write anybody or even talk to anybody.

I'm not alone with the blues either. Because of an ordnance foul-up, Joe was relieved as ordnance officer today by Jerry. Maybe he did foul up, but those measures are pretty drastic. Particularly when after dealing a guy's morale that sort of blow, you then send him into combat aviation. I hope that he doesn't let it get him down.

It's almost time to brief. And so, to war.

July 16, 1966

21:00 hours. I've been up practically all the time since midnight last night when I wrote the last entry. We briefed at 02:20 this morning, and I led Bob in on a night bombing armed reconnaissance hop. After rendezvous, we headed 301°. It was so miserably black as we approached the coast that accurate navigation was virtually impossible. Nothing can match the tension of approaching enemy shores with a definite mission, not knowing exactly where you are and not having strict control of your flight. So far, in my own judgment, I've done an excellent job of finding the right target at the right coast-in-point and delivering flares and bombs where I had intended to strike. However, I don't realize, even while I'm flying, how much the flights drain me. I come back to this damned boat, on which comfortable rest is practically impossible in the heat, and I find that my knees are almost too weak to walk. I thought it was fear, and perhaps it was fear at first, but now I'm past giving a damn if they shoot at me. Not past reasonable fear, because I'm still quite rational about the whole thing, and I don't take unnecessary chances especially with the life and welfare of my wingman. However, I'm just becoming aware that the artillery and flak, though I know they're aiming at me and trying to kill me, personally, don't intimidate me, and I can fly a good bombing pass and get good hits regardless of looking down a machine-gun barrel.

This is on the coastal Recce hops, though. Alpha strikes are another thing entirely. Today at noon, after a couple of hours' sleep, we briefed for a strike on a highway/railroad bridge just outside town, south of Hanoi. The strike was planned, but the flight didn't go. The weather was too bad. Instead we launched the strike group and struck alternate targets closer to the coast. The XO's flight hit a bridge in south Vinh. Bob and I went after Waterway number six, which is the waterway alongside Highway 1-A. We had a little better luck in this area in the daytime. We found about thirty barges, big ones, in the southern part, and with no ground fire at all we hit them again and again. There were cumulus build-ups all along the area, and we had aborted run after aborted run. I must have made twelve or fourteen passes before I expended my two MK-81's and four MK-82's. My first bomb was a dud, and what a miserable target, and no explosion. We got mostly good hits though and destroyed six or eight barges, damaged that many more, and did some slight damage to a small bridge of no strategic value along the highway. From now on, I'm going after those darned bridges, and they're coming down, safety be damned!

It's almost impossible to tell how badly you can get to wanting to do some concrete damage which you can look at and say, "There, I did that to you." And to that purpose, night flights are so tremendously exacting as to drain you of every trick, every maneuver, every device for finding an exact position and doing what you mean to do there, without killing somebody and in an orderly fashion becoming a professional soldier. There's just no way around being keyed up; that's too natural, and besides a man would have to be a fool, and probably soon be a dead one, to be careless and relaxed.

The big thing is this: YOU JUST CAN'T SEE A GOD-DAMNED MISERABLE THING. You can't see the coast, you can't see the hills, you can't see the bays, and you can't mark the flak sites, except by pure extra-sensory perception. And that's the truth. I've dropped flares when I knew I was "there" without one damned hint to back up this "knowledge," and looked down to see that I was right.

Often you come back to the ship and tell the War Room staff, "We found bad weather, headed south, found no traffic in the Ha Tinh area, and dropped our bombs on a bridge already out of commission." And that's the summary, the gist, the résumé, of two hours of pure sweat and blood, adrenalin and steel balls, to say, "We did this piddly bit," and then to walk off on shaky legs and fall across your rack for a two-hour catnap before the next thrilling go.

July 17, 1966

The XO informed me tonight that the second-in-command in the Bureau of Personnel was aboard yesterday with the DCNO, and that the skipper had spoken to him about my orders to VX-5 in September. The answer, fourthhand by now, is that it will probably be a simple thing, and one that comes about. I'll go to VX-5, but at the completion of this cruise. I don't really mind so much, but the news will be a slam to Marilyn. She'll be upset like never before. I haven't written her yet about the orders, and I think I'll wait until tomorrow. I'm just too sleepy and need the two hours' rest between now and my first hop tonight. Besides, I surely want to tell her as easily as I can.

July 18, 1966

My impatience and bad humor are going to cause me trouble with the XO and skipper.

I flew with Glenn today and was pleased at the improvement in his flight procedure, airmanship, and radio discipline. It was an uneventful hop; we found no really great targets, but we were flying in the worst weather yet. It was all milk and goo and high overcast with no light leaks to give hints of where we were, a perfect moonshiner, rum-running night. I've started carrying a tiny red-lensed flashlight to see my instruments, and I turn all my instrument and console lights completely off, even though they're red and turned down to almost nothing anyway. If they're turned off completely, sometimes starglow on the water will give you just the clue you need. I have the coastline memorized from China to the demilitarized zone. On every hop, after the mission is complete, I take my wingman and fly about ten miles to sea, up and down the coast, learning the geography, every rock, hill, and bay.

At 03:50 I took Bob out with two pods of machine guns each to reconnoiter the road about forty miles north of the DMZ. We had hoped to spot some trucks, but had no luck. Then I started a run on some barges, but broke off just before firing because I discovered that they were fishing boats. Bob spotted a big boat, about ninety feet long, and took a shot at it. All hell broke loose from just south of the waterway, some machine gunner hoping we'd miss the big target and opening up when we discovered the prize. Just then Bob lost his radio and was pursuing the run, with me screaming over the radio, "Break left, keep it turning, let's regroup over the coast, get the hell out of here!" And then I could have cried as he (knowing that nothing was wrong) calmly turned around and set up for another run. I followed at max power, rocking my wings, trying to get his attention. Finally as he approached the firing point, I ripped across in front of him, and he almost shot me down. But we made it back to the ship.

Then we made the big strike of the day. We mustered thirty-seven aircraft overhead the ship with twenty-five tons of ordnance and headed out. For twenty-three minutes there was flak, bullets, and everything that they could throw at us. I damn near blacked myself out dodging some of that garbage. At the target, our visibility was greatly reduced by flying steel.

I had a beautiful run and dropped five 1000# bombs right on that gorgeous bridge. Approaching the target, I saw two SAM's coming for us and called, "Childplay, missiles away. Break left!"

After the run, the flak was walking a steady path up my exhaust trail. I looked out to the left, and there came an F-8 hauling home. I caught in my mirror the flash of a missile, called again, and went 360° to the right, behind the hills or karst ridges. As I reversed at low altitude, I looked up to the left in time to see the missile hit the F-8, right up the intake, and the whole mess made one big ball of fire, disintegration. That was our first fatality for the cruise. That makes three shot down, and all F-8's from the same squadron.

I still haven't written Marilyn about having to stay for the whole cruise. I'm planning to ask her to fly to Manila in early September. The ship will be in port for ten days. I'll ask for leave, and I'll be able to be with her for the period when the ship is in Hong Kong as well—a grand total of three weeks. It'll be a great trip for her, and one we may never get the chance to take again, at least, not for a while.

I almost wish for her sake that I had never received the original orders. I'm really torn up inside. I belong here, and the fact that I don't like it and would rather be somewhere else shouldn't matter as much as it does. The skipper's right, the XO's right, but I had dared to hold to the idea of wrapping my arms about Marilyn in September, knowing that I wouldn't have to say good-by for years, and now I have to let that idea go. Having her over here will be expensive, but it will be worth it. Why not? Might be our only chance.

I'll write her a letter now and write my brother Easy as well. I'll ask him to call her and give her morale a boost— and ask him to urge her to meet me. She might not, thinking of all the expense and trouble, but if I know her, she'll start packing when she gets the letter.

July 21, 1966

Both my hops today were "fun" trips, except for my eyes. After a night hop and no sleep and a hard day hop, sweat poured down my forehead, burning my eyes and eyelids. I'm just plain tired after three weeks on the line.

I need to write Marilyn again right away; I know that she'll be upset about my change in orders.

I was right behind the F-8 that was shot down the other day and would have sworn that no one could have lived through all that. We heard yesterday though that a pilot was reported captured by Hanoi radio yesterday. If this is so, he's alive, and we still haven't lost a pilot in our first three weeks here.

July 22, 1966

Today I flew an Ironhand anti-SAM south of Hanoi. We held off the coast in an orbit at 8000 feet. That's an eerie feeling, just hanging out there like a decoy, knowing that there are GCI and early warning radar sites painting you and watching everything you do and that these people have the potential of launching MIG's or SAM's from almost any westerly direction from north to south. Finally I made my run. Cloud cover prevented seeing missile impact (but I'm skeptical about the results, although I made a big thing of it back in the ready room). Then we joined with Bost's section again to go inland and hit a supply storage area just south of the original target for the strike group. This, in my opinion, is pretty daring, sending one strike group in on a target, waking the enemy up, and getting them all to general quarters—then sending in another group, five minutes later while all the world is scanning the skies, hoping to find some darned American aircraft to blast at. It's like a fellow hitting a hornet's nest with a stick, then handing you the stick and saying, "Your turn, pal!" Slightly less than safe.

Though Bost was in the lead, I spotted the target first and called it, then rolled in first with Bob close behind me. Our remaining ordnance was two LAV-319-rocket pods. We each fired them, and although they all "shot-gunned" the area covering the complete hillside, we probably did no more damage than to kill whatever people were about or perhaps to chance damage supplies or vehicles. We couldn't tell. Then Bost and Jerry dropped dud bombs on the target, doing nothing more than scaring somebody, and maybe not even that.

I don't trust Don Bost's airmanship. He keeps calm in the air, but I just don't trust his judgment. When he gets duds, you can't help wondering if maybe he forgot something in the cockpit.

July 23, 1966

My first hop this morning started with a 02:25 brief. I flew Bost's wing on the dawn patrol hop. He got lost and took us between Ha Tinh and Vinh instead of the northern water-way of Brandon Bay, but I didn't recognize the area either, a risky mistake at best. We dropped a number of flares, saw nothing. Then he called out where we really were, and I remembered a truck park in the area, which we had hit on a day strike once. I threw a 250 pounder in at it and got some AAA fire or maybe 37 mm flak from our old friend on the missile site. I called it out, 360°'d right, and thought I held his position. So I put a stick of four MK-82's where I thought he was. After the last bomb, he returned fire, so I know I missed him. It's still a war of luck.

And bad luck for many. Cdr. Falcon was leading a division of A-4's in to strike a petroleum storage area just outside the city of Vinh. Vinh, halfway up the North Viet-namese coast, is one of the hottest areas of antiaircraft fire of every sort. Just the word Vinh can give me a cold hard feeling in my stomach.

Coming in from the south, from behind a small ridgeline, Cdr. Falcon led the strike group in at low altitude, climbing at the last minute for a dive-bombing attack. As they approached the target and the flak and tracers began to appear everywhere, Pat's plane in the second section was hit but not badly damaged.

During the pull-up after the diving attack, a 37 mm shell hit Cdr. Falcon's cockpit. Miraculously, the shell went right through the cockpit without exploding.

Telling the story later, Cdr. Falcon said that when he realized that he had been hit, he began moving the control stick back and forth, jinking to make himself a harder target. But he noticed that the aircraft did not respond to his maneuvering. He then saw that his hand was not on the stick at all. It was lying limp on the right console beside him. He grabbed the stick with his left hand and headed seaward, where the search-and-rescue destroyers steam up and down the coast on alert to assist downed pilots in whatever way they can. He thought about attempting a landing aboard ship, 150 miles to sea, but he saw that he was losing too much blood and was unlikely to remain conscious very long.

So he flew over the destroyer on station and ejected. The force of an ejection often injures the pilot, but to a man already seriously wounded, the G forces alone are enough to leave him unconscious.

Cdr. Falcon not only ejected with most of his right arm shot away, but parachuted into the water, got out of his parachute, and inflated his life vest. Before the destroyer could get to him, a helicopter was launched. These waters are said to be the most shark-infested in the world, and it must be true. He had hardly been in the water a minute before sharks began circling him. The helo hovered overhead, holding off the sharks with automatic rifle fire, while a small boat was launched for the pick-up. He was given first aid aboard the destroyer and flown back to the ship, where his arm was amputated.

Falcon's accident has given everyone a different twist in their bowels, a different fear. It's easier in some ways to see someone blown to bits instantly than to see a man lose an arm. I've always said it's easier to die for an ideal than to live for it. Dying takes only a moment's courage, while life is a battle against day-by-day eroding and grinding forces. To stand up to life and to hold to high standards sincerely is a more difficult price than an instant death. It's easier to go out in a glorious flaming surrender to death in favor of some cause than it is to boldly, drudgingly, daily stand up to be counted on the side of that you value most.

For me, the worst would be finding myself on the ground, captured by the NVN. That keeps me going sometimes when I don't like to think about going into the Hanoi area—the fact that maybe some imprisoned aviator will hear me down there and, to whatever degree possible, take heart.

I remember the feeling in Preflight when, as a cadet, I used to go every afternoon to the base chapel and pray alone before the evening chow call. I felt that at last all the things that I valued most in my personal life were intimately tied up in what I was doing. I need to recapture that feeling, to steel me now, especially on these night hops when all your fatigue and blue thoughts and loneliness seem to lie upon you most heavily.

This morning, on the flight deck, still black night, I thought of those guns and of the stumbling around in the dark, and I thought of a hundred reasons why I shouldn't go. I was tired and sleepy, knew that I probably wouldn't hit anything anyway, and I kept thinking of those guns and flak. But I went, and maybe I kept some VN awake and worried too. Perhaps by chance I did some damage, but I doubt it. I believe that they could move the whole NVN army down the road in four-abreast formation and I might not see them in the light of the flares we use.

July 24, 1966

Yesterday some blackshoe goof reached to punch the microphone to announce the evening prayer and punched the button for general quarters instead. [General quarters is the call for all hands to man battle stations and prepare for attack.] The gongs started sounding all over the ship; people hit the deck making like firemen getting dressed. When he said, "Disregard my last; disregard the GQ warning. Stand by for the evening prayer!" everyone had something to pray for, a prayer of thanksgiving. When you're 100-150 miles south of Red China, a call to battle stations is slightly different from a call when you're just off Mayport, Florida.

Norris got a letter from Donald Short. Don said, "Dear Norris, I don't know if you're dead or not, so I'll write this as though your parents are going to read it. On second thought, Mary will probably be the one to read it, and she's more open-minded. Dear Mary . . ."

We have steamed south in the wake of an advancing typhoon, heading for more open seas for maneuvering space. The weather isn't so bad yet that flight ops have cancelled.

We've been having a lot of trouble with the catapults. The *Sara* considered herself in real trouble when two of her four cats were down, but this tub only has two cats, just two bow cats, no waist or amidships cats. At almost every launch, one of these two has been down. Normally a launch takes from eight to twelve minutes. Night before last we were forty-five minutes getting everyone off the ship. This means you're shorted in time to get to target and complete missions. And it also means that the folks waiting to land are down to low-fuel states by the time the recovery starts.

George in the VFP squadron, the photo reconnaissance attachment, says that the staff is just guessing, that nobody really knows where the NVN store their oil. So we see a mound and say, "Yeah, yeah underground POL, hit it!" and we blow up Phu Phu Phu's burial mound or God knows what.

There's an incredible overestimation on the damage we do. It's mostly imagination or propaganda. Radio Hanoi yells about the numbers of aircraft shot down in a given day, and we laugh and call them crazy, wild propagandists. Then we tell about the bridges, trucks, barges, and POL storage areas which we've blown to hell every day, and our releases read worse than the Hanoi crap. Hell, if you took the combined estimated BDA reports from just the time we've been here, a total like that would cripple the little nation.

As Norris says, "I'd hate to be an aviator's mother back in the States reading Hanoi's evaluation of anti-aircraft successes, but I'd hate worse to be a truck driver's mother in Hanoi reading the American estimates of trucks blown up—it reads like a Detroit production figure!"

My hop for today was an easy, uneventful, tanker hop. I used to hate them, but now they provide a few peaceful, air-conditioned moments to put my brain in neutral gear and appreciate the beauty and thrill of flying without the burden of managing a flight or taking the risk of being shot. Nice.

After chow tonight, I had a three-hour bull session with Glenn. He's most different and unusual, hard to understand, yet quite mature and responsible, I think. His flying is improving. He's too easily offended by honest criticism, but most people who consider themselves good are proud. It must be tough on him being the junior man in the squadron.

July 25, 1966

Night operations were cancelled after I wrote last night. A good thing. People are really getting worn down, particularly the ordnance crews who load tons and tons of ordnance on the aircraft, reconfigure for different kinds of weapons, fix discrepancies on the ordnance gear, and catch naps as best they can, behind the island, on aircraft wings, or under the gun mounts.

What a fun day today has been! Flight ops were cancelled again today so I didn't Alpha strike it at Vinh. I started the day by sleeping from midnight till noon, straight through.

In the afternoon CAG called and said to get hold of all the squadron and have them muster down in Ready 5 at 16:00 for a mandatory medical brief. I did. When we got there, Donald had set up two big lemonade coolers, lemonade mixed with 190 proof grain alcohol from the medical supply locker. I've never seen anything like that on ship before. Both attack squadrons were smashed, from Glenn up to CAG.

At 16:45 I was ordered to break out the guitar, and we sang for three hours. The XO knows as many country songs as I do, and Edd knows more. I got too busy playing the guitar to do as much drinking as I usually do. Jack S. fell over a ready room chair, spilled juice all over himself, got another, walked back, started to sit down, fell over the same exact chair, and spilled another drink. Toward the end, Cdr. Angel called air ops on the squawk box and led a rousing verse of, "Good Morning, Good Morning, How'd You Like to Bite My Ass!" Once a call came saying, "Man aircraft," but it was only Norris using our ready room box.

July 26, 1966

Nothing happened today. I didn't even think. I got up at noon, saw a movie in the ready room, did some paper work, played gin, and ate. I drank a shot of gin in bed because my mind began playing tricks on me—asking questions and demanding answers about why I was alive and to what end and purpose was I directing my efforts, and to what extent did I size up to the measure of a man in that mind's eye of mine that keeps searching me out.

I guess I need to hate a little; to be a little more personally involved, although I never win, fighting mad. Manning aircraft at 03:30, in the black, thinking about two hours in enemy territory, weaving and searching, and all the while keeping up with the other fellow, though, sometimes requires a great deal of stamina to get my enthusiasm up; a little hate might take care of that. I know that they're shooting at me and Norris and Barry and all of us; I'm just not vindictive enough. I hope it doesn't take the loss of one of us to get me on the proper plane.

My answer to all these questions? I am ashamed to admit that I had another shot of gin and spent the rest of the night reading *Alice in Wonderland*.

July 27, 1966

I made a 10:15 brief for a hop that I'd have as soon not gone on—a strike on a petrol storage area (POL) right in the heart of Vinh. Boy, what a bad reputation that place has.

An "Old Salt" section that Jack led went in first with me leading Bob in right behind. That was an exciting few minutes. We caught them by surprise, I think, because we got no ground fire that we saw. There is a SAM site near where we bombed; missiles were fired there yesterday at some Air Force F-4's, but we received no fire.

Anyway, I rolled in like a wild man on a bronco, yanking the control pole around like it meant something to me, put my gunsight on the target, got my range and airspeed, and punched the bomb pickle to drop my four bombs. Three fell, but one 1000 pounder hung on the wing. Well, partner, in a 70° dive, pulling out at 7 G's, you don't want to have no 1000 pound asymmetric moment going against you, else you might do an unplanned maneuver and effect a rendez-vous with the dirt, fouling up your entire hop. A flash went through my mind, "I have no wing racks to bring back; I can jettison the whole kit." My mind and hand worked a little too fast, and I yanked the jettison (emergency release) handle before I remembered that it was set on "All" rather than on "Wings Only" so I dropped the bomb and along with it my centerline fuel tank, with gas in it.

By this time I was pretty near old Mother Earth, and I yanked back and got on the road east. Bob was a split second behind me and looked up just off his run. I was into the sun from him and just as he saw me, he saw my aircraft seem to split into three parts, and I was obviously not in my bombing run. The three parts were the bomb, the drop tank, and my aircraft, each taking a different flight path. He watched the drop tank instead of me, thought it was me, and got all excited. The bombs blew the heck out of the tanks, and they were still burning visibly from forty miles out to sea just before we landed.

It's time for some sleep. I need it; I'm done in. Tomorrow I'm going SAM hunting up around Hanoi again, but tomorrow after flight ops secure, we steam for Cubi Point in the Philippines for four days. We've been at sea for one month as of tomorrow. After my 20:00–24:00 watch tomorrow night, I plan to seek out Barry or Norris and set about to finish up any spare refreshments adrift about the ship.

July 28, 1966

Today we had our first aircraft downed, first aircraft for my squadron for the cruise. That damned Vinh again. Darell, Glenn, and I went in, and Glenn didn't come back. I hope that obnoxious son-of-a-gun is walking around down there somewhere, but I don't really believe it.

Darell was picking up a SAM radar and homing in on it for a missile shot when Glenn called, "Missiles away," and I heard him call again, "Keep it turning and hit the deck." We all scattered and watched the missiles explode above us. Then Darell popped back up for another shot. He fired two missiles and watched them impact: two good hits. Johnny and Harold, who were in another flight nearby, thought they heard "Maverick Two, good *chute*" on their radio, and therefore decided that someone saw a parachute. But nobody in the air would admit making the call, and we decided that perhaps Glenn had watched Darell's hits and had called, "Maverick Two good shoot" or "good shooting." It wasn't ninety seconds after Darell fired his missiles that we missed Glenn. All we really know is that his last heading was inland toward downtown Vinh.

I'm not as pessimistic about his chances as some, for if he took a hit and lost his radio, he might have glided in that direction (inland to the highlands). The hazards of ejection were less for Glenn, for he had been a paratrooper in the Army.

61

A few nights ago in our bull session, Glenn gave me a few hints about landing in water, and what you could do in addition to what we've already been taught. He feels much the same way I do about capture. Although we're taught that the best thing to do is to throw away your pistol if capture is imminent, since the NVN insist that captives go unharmed (it makes for their most effective weapon against our morale, the trials and threats to live captives), we both agreed that we would probably try to shoot it out and make like a one-man army rather than quietly march off to Hanoi.

I don't think Glenn is in pain. He's either out there evading like he's been trained to do, or he's dead, and killed quickly and without enduring much suffering. That's what I'd try: the long shot of escape, rather than the long shot of outliving and outlasting the brainwashing and rehabilitation.

What an odd place that Vinh is. Yesterday on that hop with Jack, not a shot or missile was fired. And today, no Glenn. Oh hell, you can't help hoping he's walking around down there somewhere . . . or maybe he got smart and headed for Sydney or Borneo. Not likely, but I hope so.

So last night I broke out the old guitar. A Kentucky boy on the line crew had been after me for a guitar session, and we wired our guitars through the movie projector amplifier in the ready room and had a good old Bluegrass hoedown, to the disgust of many of the city slickers aboard. I didn't give a damn for what they thought anyway. The Kentucky guy's name is Scruggs, and it's appropriate. He sang "Detroit City" and "Fireball Mail" like Nashville itself.

Glenn McWhorter, Ensign, USNR, killed or missing.

July 29, 1966

In my Preflight class, our Marine sergeant, Sgt. Morrison, was a former prizefighter, bullnecked, and the most decorated man in his outfit in Korea. He was the toughest fellow you can imagine, and the cadets ate it up, especially me. Each man was allowed to have one picture displayed in his room; four men to a room, that meant four pictures. Somehow George Bartley, one of the troublemakers in our class, got a copy of a picture of Sgt. Morrison in full-dress whites and ribbons, had a print made for every cadet in the class, and when the sergeant came up for morning room inspections, there in every room were four pictures of him displayed in very tasteful frames. He carried the matter to the battalion Marine captain, who said that there was nothing illegal about it unless the sergeant could prove that the pictures were obscene.

Sgt. Morrison was killed just outside Da Nang about six weeks ago. George told me about his death last week. George Bartley left the ship last night for Cubi Point in an A-D about midnight, and he hasn't been heard from since. He must have crashed over water and failed to eject. Both men gone.

July 30, 1966

More bad news today. We sent two of the junior officers, Ens. Worley and Lt.jg. Arrows, into the Philippines early so that they could practice landing at Cubi last night. They were to tank between bounces and inflight refuel from Don Bost, the airborne tanker. The weather was rotten, a 1000-foot overcast with mountains all around. And that ineffective, incompetent, no-brain, no-talent, worthless SOB tried to make those green nuggets in-flight refuel at night, over water, with no horizon, at *700 feet*. Need I say more? Arrows was last seen flying over a village, shortly after which a big fireball was seen 500–600 meters seaward. No way to even recover his body.

It was too bad about that incompetent; he got one killed and died too. Both of them were getting out of the Navy, and the loss was tragic for their folks and friends. I'm not God or a decent judge, but if I called merely the "good of the service" side, I'd say it was a pity that Bost didn't deep-six his own aircraft and himself along with it. When you go out with any qualified section leader, not to mention an experienced senior officer, you ought never to have to think for two people. And when folks are shooting at you, it's one hell of a time to distrust your leader. I wish someone would can Bost, ditch him, save his life, and more likely save some other people's lives at the same time. That's why sob stories about being washed out of the training command never really touched me very deeply. There's no in-between; you're either an asset, or you're one hell of a liability.

There. That's off my chest.

Barry heard Ed questioning Donald about a DFC for which he had been recommended for making a great bullpup missile strike on a couple of bridges: "Was there any flak or AAA fired at you?"

"No, not a shot."

"Well, it was in Qui Vinh, and there are many sites there; they must have been shooting at you."

"No, not a shot."

"Well, suppose we say, since there were all those sites around, and since you can't really say that they weren't shooting at you and you didn't see it, and since without resistance of a concrete nature, you'll never get this award, suppose we say in the letter of recommendation that there were heavy antiaircraft defenses, and that in the face of hostile fire, you pressed your attack and completed your mission with the threat of loss of life and without regard for your own welfare."

And Donald, thank goodness for decency, told him to go to hell and where to put his DFC.

Think about it. World War II aviators flying crates for hours over Germany, five hundred miles from home base, getting awards for really laying their life on the line, and we fictionalize to get the same award. No thanks.

I plan to make it up to the mountains for the next two days and R&R by doing some serious sleeping and loafing. Also plan to call my sweet wife.

August 5, 1966, en route to Yankee Station

We're returning from a much needed rest. I've spent the last four days swimming, loafing, fishing, and sleeping, trying to get back in shape.

In port at the Naval Station at Cubi, Cdr. Falcon was relieved of command. He stood, the empty right sleeve of his dress whites pinned to his shoulder, and read his orders. After the ceremony, refusing assistance, he walked down the gangway, weaker toward the last but refusing help, and got into an ambulance waiting there to take him to the base hospital. I know that I'll remember his show of strength.

Lots of old friends were in Cubi Point. Gerald Marshall showed up, and I had dinner with him. Gerald has real doubts about our part in the war here and is having a problem deciding what to do. I told him to turn in his wings and get the devil out; he's worthless in his current state of mind. Steve Ellison is his skipper and is as right-wing as anyone can get. If Gerald tries to push for a transfer because of his belief that our involvement in Vietnam is wrong, he may wind up with a court-martial from Cdr. Ellison. His only out is to turn in his wings and that means an end to his flying. Some people who were eating with us were ready to hit Gerald. I just went to bed feeling a little uncertain myself and dejected.

My treat of treats for the in-port period was to call Marilyn. How great to talk to her! My emotions first said, "Why the hell did she say, 'I'm coming to meet you if you want me'?" For a minute I felt so small, so completely distant, inadequate, and isolated, but then my brain engaged and I thought, "She's like you, idiot, she occasionally needs reassuring too."

When we get to Hong Kong, I'm going to get a room with a giant bathtub, fill it with warm water, and we'll soak all afternoon, like a couple of otters. Otters in love.

I want to repay her in some small way for being so near to me out here, but it'll only be a small token. On second thought, I don't want to repay her in any way, what I want is to hold her, close my eyes, and know that when I waken, she'll still be there the way I love her most, drowsy and loving and warm and soft and lovely. That's what I want, and it's all for myself. It won't be long, but it can't be soon enough.

I wrote Marilyn a three-page letter saying much of the above and a lot of other endearing things which I meant but didn't say too well. As I was finishing the letter, Norris came in, and we talked a few minutes about Mary and Marilyn, and how we need to keep them reassured. Norris has found the same thing true about Mary, but Mary is more aggressive than Marilyn and lets him know when she is feeling neglected.

August 8, 1966

I took Bob through a damned reckless bombing spree north of Vinh day before yesterday, and as irony would have it, we put our bombs right on the trenches of oil drums, and a big press release went out last night about it. Our flying was stupid, careless, and bullheaded; our hits were sheer luck.

We went in low over the water, heavy as hell, sooner than we should have gone in on a one-shot deal. As it worked out, hitting the coast at the waterway south of Brandon Bay and popping up to 4000–5000 feet, instead of having 400 knots, we had about 300—too damned slow for that part of the country. Then to make matters worse I went in a little too far south, and instead of shading the target to the north, I saw it almost directly under me at 10:00 low. So I wingovered high and pulled a lot of G's to get turned 180° around and bled off more precious airspeed. In my run I was so damned slow that when I tried a 4-G computer release, I stalled and stalled, fell and fell.

I finally got out at 1200 feet, vulnerable to anything from cannons to cornstalks, slow as a snail, and right in the frag pattern of my own bombs. The concussions shook my whole aircraft, and it's a wonder I got out. But the NVN must have been asleep. Bob rolled in behind me and got off a good volley of bombs. He saw mine hit on target and looked back to see his own bombs hit the target. There were oil fires for thirty minutes after the strike.

Good flying? The world's worst; success seems to be more and more a matter of luck.

I find I react to all kinds of things when I'm in the air. If I've eaten a good meal before a flight, I can tell the difference in increased stamina and the speed of my reactions. If I haven't eaten well, I'm weak by the time I land on board ship.

Marilyn's letters affect me too. Yesterday I received the poem which she had written on the thirty-first. I read it, leaned back, closed my eyes, and smiled, read it again, thought of all I have to live and be thankful for, suited up, went out, and gave 'em hell!

I hit the Red River and roared in almost to downtown Haiphong with Ralph on my wing. We received a warning that MIG's were coming after us. I swung south and on the way out found some barges on our alternate route. I let discretion go for a moment and hit them with rockets on the way out. Then the "Cottonpicker," Air Force radar jammers and radar warning aircraft, said more MIG's were taking off and SAM radars were tracking us. We made it to the coast just before the bad guys got there and headed out.

Ralph thought we were on the way home, but we still had four bombs each. Twenty-five minutes to landing time, and I headed south along the coast to where Darell had found some heavily defended supply areas around Vinh, flying over the dreaded Song Ca waterway and headed max thrust toward downtown Hell. There went the bombs, and here came the flak. Good hits on the bombs; lucky misses on the flak. I got Ralph back at critical low fuel state. For once I felt that I had flown a hop worthy of the risk involved.

And mostly thanks to Marilyn's poem. A large part of the joy and pain of her is in the necessity I feel to be worthy of her.

Sleep, or lack of sleep I should say, is the other factor which seems to affect my flying most. We're flying noon till midnight now, and I'm in good shape, but I don't even like to think about those sleepless days when we're flying at night. That's when I'm least safe in the air.

August 9, 1966

Today is the third day on the line since our short break at Cubi Point in the Philippines.

Last night I had a hell of a time getting to sleep. It was feverishly hot in my rack, and I kept getting up and lying down. I started going to bed about 19:00 and must not have gone to sleep until after 01:00.

The XO and Johnny just left on an Ironhand for Richard's and Tim's strike on a POL near Thanh Hoa. Darell and Benny, Bost and Ralph are taking two sections out for armed reconnaissance along Hon Me, inland where some cars are reportedly on the railroad tracks, and where Darell yesterday found what he thinks might be a truck park.

I have the duty and am smoking a long black Marsh Wheeling that Benny said someone gave him. I rather suspect they were Joseph Arrows's. On that subject, night before last, Richard, Darell, and I met informally in Richard's room and talked about the accident. We will write the final report for the accident board. We are all trying not to be prejudiced against Don Bost, and yet everyone knows what a complete ineffective he is. Consequently we have probably said too little and been too lenient in an effort to be objective. One sentence in the report says that "the judgment to expect an inexperienced pilot to effect a rendezvous at 700 feet, at night, under an 800-foot overcast, with no definite horizon, is considered unsound." Richard suggested that we change the word *unsound* to *insane,* which better voices what we all feel. Still, this is how the report will doubtless go—unsound. That's about as mildly as it can be said.

No more Dixie Station; the Air Force now has South Vietnam, and the big boys get handed the dirty work. The *Intrepid,* formerly Dixie-only carrier, is now in company with us, and the *Constellation* is here on Yankee. She's daylight only while the rest of us alternate in twelve-hour shifts, changing at noon and midnight.

Day before yesterday we lost a spad, shot up over Cape Felice. The pilot made it to water but lost control and crashed in the water while still aboard. On that same day the Air Force lost five F-105's; three were shot down in that valley of death west of Hanoi, and the other two crashed into the water off Haiphong. We got no battle

report on those two, and we assume it was a midair colli-
sion or an operational accident. Hell of a day. And yesterday the *Intrepid* lost an A-4, a tanker who flew into the
water in the landing pattern.

August 10, 1966

I'm getting dangerous, I guess. I'm more and more tempted
to press attacks more closely, hit harder, go lower for ac-
curacy. I guess if it were not for the responsibility of a
wingman I'd be doing all these things. But it would bother
me to get someone else in trouble in defiance of standard
operating procedure, and that's been a big defense mecha-
nism for me; that of all the people I know who have been
killed in aircraft accidents, none were because I got them in
trouble or failed to do or say something I should have.

It's been gratifying (but always only when back on the
ground) that on probably no less than 85 per cent of all the
hops I've gone on, I've been the flight leader, almost always
again, though, on a two-plane strike.

Since there are usually two or more flights of "Magic
Stone" in the air at once, the more junior flight has to get
another voice call. Mine has finally really solidified, and I'm
"Genghis One," and whoever flies with me naturally ex-
pects to be "Genghis Two." Some Air Force pilots have
heard us and commented once at Cubi that we were using

an original call. The call was originated by Bob and his "Genghis Khan" nickname for my mustache. The Air Force pilots saw the mustache and understood. Big fun.

August 13, 1966

I'm grounded with a cold and doped up with medicine.

Last night Barry, flying on the skipper's wing, found the barges in company with that Russian freighter, having been refueled, being towed away in a trail of three, by a big tugboat. Barry laid a stick of bombs right on target and left two of the petrol-laden barges burning for two hours, visible at the ship from 20,000 feet, 140 miles away. As much as the captain and admiral have been under pressure to get those barges and not damage the Russian boat, Barry will get a hero's medal for sure, and far more important than that, really deserves one. That probably thwarted a week's work by that crew up there and again hit at their petrol supplies. Proud of that Barry, a Carolina boy.

I've been lying here thinking about North Carolina. I remember I used to be so proud of my daddy, because he was the most intelligent man I knew—nobody had to tell me and nobody had to be told—and because he was so physically strong and daily proved it by outworking the rest of us in the field and around the barns, on the ditchbanks and in new ground. I used to also be proud of him because he never let me get close enough to love him. I was always sure he didn't like me too much, but still I was his and he was mine, and being the man I thought he was, that was better than having anyone else I could think of for a father. He was that. He was more a father than a daddy.

My daddy was my Uncle Gaston. Before I was old enough to go to school, he started letting me ride his old gray mule. I don't ever remember not riding "Old Gray" through the tobacco fields. Hitched to a rough pine sled we called a drag, he would giddap and whoa, giddap and whoa, down a furrow between two rows of tobacco while the croppers gathered the ripe leaf.

Uncle Gaston used to tell me about my older brother's boyhood because he knew that more than anything else I wanted to be like him. My brother was twelve years older than I, but Uncle Gaston had stored in the attic of the old home place where he lived most of Lloyd's old *Boys' Life* magazines, and I remember looking through them when I was about the age for Boy Scouts.

The whole house was, as it had always been, unpainted flat pine. Uncle Gaston's room had been his parents', my grandparents', lit earliest in my memory by a kerosene lamp and later by a single light bulb that hung by the wire down to and just out-of-reach above the head of his bed. He could turn the light out by pulling a hemp string tied to the bead chain pull-switch of the fixture.

I used to sleep in the second bed there when I spent the night with him. He was the kindest gentleman in my memory, perhaps because I never thanked him for his kindness in any way that could justify it to me . . . that's not what I want to say. I never did thank him enough while he was alive, but maybe there's an unspoken thanks that means more between a man and a boy than any other kind.

He was my mother's brother. He had gone to State College at one time, had never married, had never acquired a lot of land or money, and to my young eyes had absolutely no faults. He drank beer, I believe, because he was lonely and because there was a lot he had missed in life. But he never grumbled that I remember. He merely led an everyday, obscure, humble, unhappy life, and gave me the grandfather I never had and replaced that part of my own father's life that was not then available to me.

I don't remember much about his dying. I had grown out of the honesty of early boyhood into the immaturity of adolescence. I remember I cried bitterly, but some of my crying I can almost be sure was for my never having taken grasp of all he had to give and teach me. I miss him now when I see my father reach the age that he too wants to give me something, wants me to take something of his on with me, wants to communicate something to me I cannot know otherwise . . . something of that nature was forever cut off from me when Uncle Gaston died.

August 15, 1966

Day before yesterday I was racked out in sick bay watching Arthur Godfrey, who was aboard ship to open our new closed-circuit TV station. I had managed to get a room in the isolation ward, all to myself, nice and cold.

Suddenly Maverick One brought me a drink of some 200 proof stuff mixed with Hawaiian Punch that was being served at a "medical brief" in the wardroom. (It was the night before a stand-down, a day off, and we usually get the squadrons together in a ready room for some booze and good fellowship since we won't be flying the next day.) I heard "Well, hello Maverick Three, get th' hell up!" I looked up and there were the other Mavericks; the squadron was in the mood for a sing and wanted a guitar. I got up there and played while everyone sang, stoned to a man. Of course Arthur Godfrey was there. And drinking Lipton tea never put a man in his condition. He said later that from now on he'd worry about the morale of the civilians back home.

The rest of the evening I must put together piecemeal, mostly by sketchy memory and hearsay. I remember some wrestling, and I remember slipping and falling near the amidships bomb elevator on the hangar deck. I missed a letter which Marilyn had written me on August 4. I had to have that letter, found the letter somehow, read the letter, and went to sleep.

When I woke up the next day I felt like pure hell! I still had my cold, and my left shoulder was wrenched and my right knee, it seems, was either broken, sprained, or terribly bruised. I couldn't bend my knee, and I couldn't raise my left arm. Barry came to see me and insists that I was so far gone that I took a shower while I was still wearing infirmary pajamas.

I'm really ashamed of all this, but I don't want to color it in the account, since I'll later like to remember it as it was, good or bad. If I had to do it again, I'd stay in bed.

So tonight I have the duty and won't fly again until tomorrow. It's been some day.

August 17, 1966

Back in the flying business today. To break me in properly, I started off with two night hops, completing both before dawn this morning.

Now that it's over, I can admit it; for the last week, having that cold and feeling miserable most of the time and getting little sleep, I have had a continuing dread of night flying. Damn, did I dread it. Night flying can lie heavy on your mind anyway, but just during the last week or so, it was worse than ever.

I still have a cold left, and my right knee's still in an elastic bandage, but Bob and I really did some good on our hops. We knocked out a new pontoon bridge and set fire to a supply area on the first go, and on the second we knocked out another smaller bridge and got eight or ten barges along the waterway.

August 19, 1966

This morning on the flight deck it was 83 degrees, and people were smiling because that was the first time, day or night, that the temperature has dropped below 87 degrees tell you, you can almost faint when you're sitting on the flight deck waiting for launch time, behind another aircraft and in his jet exhaust, and your canopy is closed making yourself a nice cozy greenhouse in addition to the heat from the other fellow's exhaust. Even at night, you almost get nauseated just before launch time. After your cat shot, the first thing you do is get the air conditioner going, take off your hardhat (despite the rules and the engine noise), dry off your eyes and head, wipe the sweat out of your oxygen mask, and then settle down to business. The sweat always gathers in your eyebrows, and the force of the cat shot throws stinging sweat into your eyes.

These are the things that drive you nuts, more than getting shot at.

It's really rotten. By the time I strapped in last night, I was nauseated. I really didn't want to go. I kept thinking, man, you'll never hack a career of this! Lead a flight? You ought not even be going on this hop. And the darned cat shots, when you're nervous and it's blacker than a well with no horizon, they're something out of Edgar Allan Poe.

I've started trying to get at least a couple of hours' sleep right in the ready room in a chair, every day, to supplement the restless hours I spend in my hot room in bed. At night, I undress, wet a towel with the lukewarm water that comes out of the cold water tap, spread it over myself in the bed, and turn on the fan. The evaporation keeps me cool for a couple or three hours until the towel dries. Then I get up, get a drink of water out in the passageway to replace all the sweat I've lost, wet the towel, and try to sleep again.

I've noticed that as officers grow more senior, they forget (honestly forget, not just disregard) the things that really bugged them as junior officers. Particularly commanding officers. So I am writing down every really notable thing that I honestly feel should be done in cases where something else was done. And the main entries all have to do with the daily comfort and living standard of the crew. Some fellows have only half a rack. That is, while they work another fellow sleeps in the bed. Then shifts change, and co-owners of racks switch places.

What makes it worse is that some of the senior officers, out to make a name for themselves, make conditions even worse than they have to be. For instance, the chief engineer refused to take on a supply of water from an oiler who was on her way back into port where water is just pumped aboard. He argued that it was a point of pride that the *Oriskany* should always make her own water and supply herself. So now we're on water hours. You can only take showers at particular times of the day, though you may finish flying and be completely dirty and tired and sweaty at another time. If you're on the flight deck crew and you work during all the water hours, well, you just stay dirty.

Back at Cubi Point, one of the things we all did was to take hour-long showers. While we were dressing, we let the showers run just for the luxury of wasting water.

Cdr. Stone is really uncanny in the way he can find things that most of us don't spot, hidden trucks and boats, camouflaged barges that to me just aren't visible.

Another Stone, skipper of the A-D squadron, is just unbelievably daring. The A-D's, since they're props, do the mission of "RESCAP," rescue combat air patrol. When a pilot is shot down and is sighted as alive on the ground, they fly cover for him until the helo can get in and get him out if he's in a position where rescue is possible. Cdr. Stone, in fighting off ground troops advancing on the downed pilot, has brought back planes with rifle bullets all through the fuselage and grass stain on the propeller from tall grass and tree foliage he's flown through in a rage to keep the troops back. He's a real terror. It's nice and comforting though. Everybody that's gone down and come back so far has said they weren't really too worried when they saw the A-D's, since they knew that if it were humanly possible they'd be rescued. And most of them are. And that takes some gutsy helo pilots too to go in deep into enemy territory in a noisy, 50 mph machine with gunfire and SAM's and flak and MIG's all around.

August 21, 1966

No mail from Marilyn in almost a week now, but I'm sure it's just the routing over here. I'll probably get a bagful tomorrow.

I've asked permission to fly commercially to Hong Kong after we leave the Philippines, instead of riding the ship for that two-day trip. If that comes through, it'll mean I'll have a couple of more days with Marilyn.

Bost and his stupidity got us another airplane busted up, about 150 holes in the bottom of the aircraft when a shell hit the drop tank and exploded. Thank goodness he was in it. Bad luck for the Navy though, he got back. When you're going into the hot places, you go tearing in and try to surprise them and get the heck out before the gunners get their range. The big zero was in there making multiple runs right in the middle of a complex of flak sites, putting himself at the mercy of any hamfisted gunner able to point a sight. And, worse, he was making his wingman do likewise. Of course, most wingmen in the squadron have learned that in flying with Bost, one has to think and act for oneself, and if you get chewed out at the brief, you have the consolation of being alive and the added consolation of knowing that whatever your decision, right or wrong, it is doubtless better than Bost's standard indecision. If the shell had hit anywhere but in the drop tank, there'd be no Bost around to complain about.

Bob and I have had some pretty accurate flak and tracers coming at us lately, but no hits. I've been feeling so much better about my bombing hits that I've become less frightened. I think, to a great degree, I'm getting used to being shot at. That's probably the worst thing that could happen. An aviator is supposed to be most dangerous when he has between 600 and 1000 flight hours, when he's got his wings and finished the RAG, the Replacement Air Group, where he receives specialized training for his particular aircraft, and he's really getting comfortable in the air and willing to take chances, but he's still inexperienced. I guess I'm just about to that stage in the combat business. I don't really know what I'm doing yet except in theory; I'm still taking the brief to the target and acting out a prerehearsed scene rather than doing a naturally smooth thing. But this week things are beginning to seem easier, so I guess I'll have to watch myself to keep from getting careless.

Jerry and I had a low overcast on our flight today. The trouble with a low overcast is that you give the fellow on the ground a simple problem of range. A duck hunter who's always switching from ducks to geese has a hard time because he can't tell if it's a goose up high or a duck down low because of the difference in size of the two birds. An antiaircraft gunner has the same problem when he's firing visually; he can't tell if you're an F-8 at 12,000 feet, an A-4 at 9,000 feet, or an A-3 at 14,000 feet. But, if he can look up and see a 5000-foot overcast, he knows immediately that for anything he sees at all, he'll have an exact gauge of range.

So Jerry and I went in fast as the devil, spotted the bridges, and made our one run each, simultaneously. But holy hell, did we ever get shot at. Mostly bullets, not a lot of flak. But bullets everywhere. That fellow, or rather those fellows, really had the gauge; they were all over us. We could see where the bullets were coming from on the very top of a small hill, but we weren't about to hit back. On the way out, we headed south and looked for stuff on the wooden bridges along the highway. Then we began to get low on fuel, and I had to get rid of the stuff somewhere. I had an alternate target that was suitable, but not very juicy. So, half-jokingly, I called Jerry and said, "How about going back into Qui Vinh for another try?" I figured he'd want no part of it.

But he said, "Hell yes, I'll go anywhere you will!" Ah, sweetness, how I love to hear somebody say that! How suddenly joyful and playful it all is. You almost hope they shoot at you so you'll have a good game. We went back in, and shoot they did! Same scene all over again; zip, zip, all around us, little specks of fire zipping by us. But we put holes in both the other bridges so that a train couldn't cross town when we left. Qui Vinh is a railroad center, so the folks in AI and strike center were pretty happy when we got back. The skipper told us we were crazy for going in there, and then smiled to let us know that he was glad we went.

August 22, 1966

I wrote the watch bill for the time we're in port today. Naturally I took care of myself. Here's how it stands. Everybody has to stand one in-port SDO and one in-port integrity watch. Since it's about a six-hour bus ride from Manila to Cubi and another six back, I decided to give myself my watches in Hong Kong, where it's only a forty-five-minute boat ride from the beach to the ship. Also, I'll doubtless be able to get a standby sometime that night when some of the others get back from liberty, and that way I'll get to spend all the nights ashore with Marilyn.

My official period of leave is now the first three days in Cubi and the last three days in Hong Kong. The rest of the time I'll be on call and sort of in emergency contact only. That means that even while not on leave, I can be with Marilyn in Manila or Baguio or anywhere as long as nothing comes up that Tim can't handle for me.

I got permission to fly commercially to Hong Kong intead of having to ride the boat. That's two, almost three, days more that we can be together, from the fifth to the twenty-second or twenty-third almost continuously. That won't be nearly long enough, but it'll surely be a wonderful little bit.

Haven't had a letter from Marilyn in a week now, but I guess it's the airline strike. Glad that thing's over. Hope I get a stack of letters tomorrow.

August 23, 1966

Yahoo! Letters from Marilyn. But otherwise today has been shitty.

How is this for a day? On the first hop, Jan of VF-111 ejected from his F-8 just a little off the cat, engine trouble, compressor stalls, probably more work of the same guys who bent our aircraft. Then the terror of flying, not really knowing if something exotic was wrong with the aircraft that would only show up after you got deep into North Vietnam.

After I was launched for my second hop, the flight that was recovering as we went out was coming aboard. As an F-8 landed, the arresting wire broke and went flying, whip-lashing down the flight deck. A friend of mine (casual ward-room acquaintance), Roy, a ship's company Lt.jg., big, broad-shouldered, rugged, good-looking fellow, and his first-class ordnanceman were standing just forward of the island. The cable cut off both the AO1's legs and cut off Roy's right leg just below the knee. Horrible. Roy must have been in pure agony, and yet the only thing he kept insisting, even as they were taking him to sick bay, was that they should not tell his wife by telegram. She's to have a child in a couple of weeks. So they didn't, and he was flown off to the hospital at Saigon later today. I guess they'll let him call her later.

My second hop was up at Cac Ba or Hon Gay, the island area just south of the Chinese border. As we were leaving we got warnings of SAM radars and MIG's approaching the area. Our next flight up there got SAM's and MIG's after them, but Bob and I got there first and got the heck away at just the right time.

At 14:00 I was called into the skipper's room. He assigned four other officers and me to search the whole crew's lockers and personal belongings for dope. Narcotics. At about 08:00 this morning, two or three of our ordnancemen were found wandering around the flight deck completely hopped up on some Oriental capsules called Red Devils, pure narcotics, probably got them in Japan or the Philippines. Those things are so impure that there are frequent cases of death or insanity caused by them. And here are the ordancemen who load our bombs, on whose competency you place the bet of your very life in addition to the mission you set out to do. Here are these men wandering around drunk, or hopped up, eyes dilated as big as night. One was stopped just as he was about to walk off the flight deck. Another fell off the flight deck into the catwalk and was injured. And that's how I spent the afternoon. With all the squadron chiefs around, we searched every man's locker and sea bag. Found nothing yet, but I hope we do.

Everything's all right now. I'm not going out till daylight tonight, and I'm not frightened or jumpy or nervous. But I can't forget how Marilyn and the good Lord were (and certainly will be again) the only comfort in the world when it's black and lonesome, and people are really trying everything they know to kill you. Funny, I don't think about the personal aspect of it. Bob and I found some trucks this morning after we left Cac Ba and went hunting on our own. We turned one over and left four burning and exploding, but you only think about trucks and supplies and not people. It's cruel, but it's almost necessary to keep yourself sane if you have any humanitarian sensitivities.

August 24, 1966

Once I got to sleep yesterday, I dreamt and tossed and rolled. I had a dream about some girl I didn't know. I don't seem to dream about Marilyn that much. I guess, regardless of what else may be said, Barry is right in that man, in the primitive state at least, is not a monogamous creature. But if I found it necessary to look for other women here, loving Marilyn the way I do, and knowing that she is mine only, I couldn't get up in the morning. . . . It's not a moral thing with me; I just don't want to disappoint Marilyn in any way, don't want any secrets to come between what we share.

One thing that's really difficult about being married to her is that my attitude is now not as good as it was when I felt that I had nothing really to lose. I enjoy living more than some, and if I'm killed, surely there are plenty who will say, "Too bad," and mean it. But I've never felt that the world would be greatly altered. I've lost that attitude, though it's the best possible frame of mind to be in when you know there's a good chance you won't make it back. It's those who have too much to live for; they're always the ones who get it. And me, I've got too much to live for now. I have to keep my longings and daydreams in check, or I'm afraid I'll lose something that's really necessary to get me through all this.

After 23:00 I was half awake. I had already checked the schedule and knew where my 03:00 strike would be. Checking the schedule is always a mistake. If you don't know where you're going on a hop, you can't really worry because you can't form pictures of the terrain and the flak and the hills where you might be forced to parachute down in the pitch, milky black. But I had seen the schedule, and I knew that I was to go into the area of heavy fire at checkpoint 32 in the middle of Brandon Bay, to follow the roads west for twenty miles, then turn north and reconnaissance that part of the road up to checkpoint 38, then turn back southeast to the coast.

Lying there in bed, I mentally dodged bullets and shells, called Bob a hundred times giving him instructions, and struggled the way one will do in a dream when he doesn't know what he's fighting; I just tense up against whatever it is I'm to go up against, although tensing up doesn't do anything either. I lay there for half an hour doing this, the way in the afternoons in high school before a night football game, I would lie upstairs and mentally make touchdowns and fantastic razzle-dazzle football plays. Except in this case there was the tough load of having to shepherd Bob in and out of there as well as just live through the whole thing. And, unlike the football game, there's no great thrill about looking forward to a night armed reconnaissance hop; there's only the dread of the dark, of not seeing anything worth bombing and yet risking your very ass every minute of the night, keeping track of yourself and another man over hostile territory, making bombing runs when a mistake in navigation might drive you into a mountain or hillside, or, even easier, cause you to drop a bomb where the elevation puts you down in your own bomb fragmentation pattern and blow yourself out of the air. Hell, even night hops in the States were dangerous, and people flew into the ground and killed themselves, just because there's so damned much that you have to take care of, keep track of, and get done.

But, add all this to a murky, milky, black night, with no horizon and rolling variable terrain, and lights out in both aircraft, bullets, flak, the possibility of SAM's and MIG's, a wingman who, even though I think he's the damned best in the squadron except for Barry, is nevertheless the section leader's responsibility, and then, take all that to bed with you when you know you've got to get up in a couple of hours, right in the middle of the night, and face all that garbage. Try to get a little rest under those circumstances.

I gave up and wrote Marilyn a letter instead.

After the hop is over and you are back on the ship, it's virtually impossible to remember how much you dreaded going out there at night. It's true; even now I can't really put myself in the helpless, inadequate mood I was in before manning aircraft this morning.

During the brief in Air Intelligence, you know you're going and you listen carefully. Then back in the ready room, you begin to dread it and you go on briefing though, even though you're beginning to look for a way out, to hope that you're really not going out, that the spare will be launched in your place, that you'll be late starting, that you'll have no radio, or a bad ALQ, or something—anything—that'll give you a decent, honorable out of that particular night hop. After the brief, waiting to suit up and man aircraft, you really dread it most then. A cup of coffee and another nervous call to the head, and you're told to man your aircraft for the 03:00 launch.

Up on the flight deck, you start looking for something wrong; you go all the way around the aircraft, looking for that little gem that'll be reason enough to your conscience and your comrades to refuse to go out. And it doesn't come. You never give up though, first the damned radio works, and the damned ALQ works, and the damned tacan works. . . .

August 25, 1966

It's 08:00; at 02:30 I briefed Bob Smith and the spare, Darell, for a night armed reconnaissance hop. At 04:00 we manned aircraft. At 04:00 Bob was launched, and as I was taxiing up on the cat, I noticed his aircraft, at about one-half a mile forward from the ship, start a hard left turn.

Then I noticed he was descending rapidly, and I grabbed for the mike key. I couldn't say a word before aircraft, bombs, and everything hit the water and went up in a 1500-foot fireball. No ejection. No chance for survival.

There was no horizon, clouds everywhere, perfect vertigo weather. I suspect that this is what happened. Disorientation or a bad gyro.

Since then I've been in sort of a daze. I guess, flying with Bob every day, I got to be much closer to him than I had meant to be. Also, he was really my first wingman, and there's a lot to that too. Sort of like he was mine. And he was really coming along too. He was as good as anybody I ever met at that experience level. Gone. What a waste.

He has a kid brother aboard who is an enlisted man. I went down with the chaplain and told his brother about Bob's death this morning. He looked so sad. I finished and went out on the catwalk and cried for five minutes or so.

And the war goes on. I flew my second hop. I guess if the spare hadn't been down, I'd have been expected to fly the one on which Bob was killed. On the second hop Bob and I were scheduled to go out again. Richard was in his place. When I went back to the ready room, I expected to see Bob there ready to brief. Damn it all, it's just too bad. Engaged and to be married the first couple of weeks back from this damned place. Zap. Over. Gone. Written off.

It's a tough blow. I liked Bob, and he was so doggoned good in the air. We really didn't pal around much on the ground, but oh what a pleasure to fly with him on my wing. He held the tight formation just like I do with three years' less experience than I have. And he used his head and could be trusted. We were just getting so we could feel what the other was thinking and doing in the air. Lately, almost nothing had to be said, for we each already knew what to expect from the other. And now it's gone, and I don't think it'll ever be exactly the same. At least not this cruise. Oh God, what a loss to the squadron, to his girl, to his brother and family.

August 27, 1966

I don't like to admit this, and if I get killed and Barry reads this as I have given him permission to do, I think it may make him cringe as it would me if I were reading the same thing in his journal. However, the truth is, I downed an aircraft on deck for a bad gyro, and it just wasn't the truth.

It was a 23:00 brief with Ralph and Bost as spare. I briefed for a flight in the area of north Brandon Bay, following the route over to checkpoints 38 and up to 41. We were to look for traffic on the road. I intended to go, for I knew after having seen Bob go in the night before, I needed to have a terrifically hard hop turn out successfully before I could have my confidence restored. I intended to go, but the dread of it was in my mind all the time. When we manned aircraft at 01:00, I began meticulously looking for something wrong with the aircraft, but there was nothing really wrong.

I started, checked and rechecked everything, and everything was still working. Going through my mind right then was all the camaraderie that Barry, Tom, T.R., and I have had about not giving a damn when the going got rough and when things were most hairy, and how that what I really wanted from God right then was not the strength to endure, but just a good, safe way out. I did wrong; I can't feel any other way about that. But my conscience hasn't bothered me like I thought it might. I called, "416, in and up," and I thought that I had my head problem solved and that I was going out and solve my lack of confidence right then.

But as I taxied up on the cat, I looked to 10:30/11:00 and thought I could see Bob's lights zooming by and the fireball blazing and blinding. I couldn't see the horizon and I tried to concentrate on checking my instruments and take-off checklist. But right then, without thinking or anything else, I called, "This is 416, on Cat #2. I'm down. Bad gyro." I chickened out and didn't fly.

I flew the second hop of the day, and put a big hole in a bridge near Cao Bang.

All this happened yesterday.

Today, I briefed at 01:00 with the XO as his wingman on the same route I was to fly last night when I showed yellow. When we got to the aircraft, it was last night's scene all over again. Scared. Dread was engulfing me. No horizon. But, knowing that things weren't going to get any better until I had gone out on just such a night as this—thunderstorms everywhere, fog, soup, rain, no horizon—I wouldn't be up to myself again. So, taxiing up on the cat, there was Bob's fireball again, looking at me from 10:30, but I gritted my teeth and went ahead. Tearing down that cat, I was 100 per cent adrenalin. I ran my seat down and was all instruments and no visual. I got into the air okay, and suddenly I knew I had it made, faced the devil and grinned him down.

The rendezvous was blacker'n ever and in the goo and hairy again, but I never really sweated it. I got on the XO's wing, and here we went. Terrible weather, but I was suddenly all guts. North Vietnam couldn't get to me since I had beaten the Frank Elkins devil. I overcame the weakling, the mama's boy, the guy about whom Billy said, "Give the ball to Elkins. He'll dance across the goal." And I didn't give one rat's ass if the whole world was shooting at me, I had already won.

Fritz had an electrical failure, and after one try for the deck, punched out. He was being rescued as we were landing.

Then I heard Maverick Two call, "This is Magic Stone 403. I've lost you in the clouds, Darell."

Darell said, "Roger, make a 20° right turn." He did and the ship had him on radar and was talking to him.

Then Benny called, "I've lost my gyro and external lights."

Darell said, "Roger. Pull your emergency generator."

"Roger, but I don't think it'll do any good; I've still got my standby gyro, and I've got it under control."

"Roger. As long as you've got control."

But Benny lost the rest of his gear, lost his lights, calmly took off his kneeboard, and sold the aircraft to the fish. Bingo. Pop-up and out into the free airstream for a nylon letdown into the salt-water bath. The helo got him out after half an hour or so. He's okay, and I'm taking him on two hops tomorrow.

Since Bob's death, I've decided to retire the "Genghis" flight call—that'll be mine and his. I was "Genghis One" and Bob was "Genghis Two," and there won't ever be another "Genghis" flight as far as I'm concerned.

This week has been like a bad dream. Since Bob got killed, the whole squadron seems different to me. Never knew I thought so much of Bob. Never realized how comfortable I was flying with him, and probably I did better not to know. Damn, I never meant to let myself get close to anybody out here where a death is something you have to expect and prepare for. But without knowing it, I guess I did.

August 28, 1966

Cdr. Stone of the spad squadron just had an engine fire and jumped out at Hon Me. He was fired upon during the rescue operation, but nobody else was hurt. He was banged up a little and burned, but he's being flown back here right now. That makes nineteen airplanes we've lost in actual combat operations, not to mention the other crunches.

My own flights were uneventful: I'm beginning to recover from that bout I was having with my nerves.

August 29, 1966

Bad news today. We'll be extended on the line until September 8, which means I won't be seeing Marilyn until the ninth.

Along with the announcement night before last that we would be extended, they gave us a sort of conciliatory boon; we were given three days as white carrier. That is, we fly days only for three days, until the first. Red, white, and blue carriers; white has the day shift, blue flies noon-to-midnight, and red has the gruesome midnight-to-noon shift.

Late this evening I went out with Bost for a typical no-control, no-plan, confused two hours of pure hair, up in the island area to the north, just south of China. On earlier flights, SAM's had been fired at everyone in that area. That damned Bost had us going around at 10,000 feet, right in the most vulnerable area, at the most vulnerable altitude. We were looking for SAM sites and, boy, I got a full half hour of eye strain, not to mention mental indigestion. We drew a lot of fire from an automatic gun site. I saw two tracers fly over my right wing and then a couple go under the wing. There's a tracer bullet about every eighth round in the ammo belt; at least that's the way we did it in the North Carolina National Guard. So, for every tracer bullet you see, there are seven or so more invisible bullets zigging

97

around. The tracer helps the gunner see where he's shooting, and, incidentally, gives the aviator a sporting chance, not to mention a little fear.

Dammit, I don't feel right saying, "Come on, September ninth." It should be September fifth.

September 4, 1966

Yesterday was an eventful day for me.

Tim asked me the night before if I minded being sent into the dreaded island area around Cac Ba, Hon Gay, and the Haiphong harbor channel area on Bost's wing. That's like asking a turkey on Christmas Eve if he minds laying his head on the block of wood while you're filing your ax.

I said something like, "Hell yes; it might save some lesser wingman's life, so I'll go." But when it came time to go, I began to wish I had uttered sentiments similar to other junior officers who have flown that particular tactical position.

We accompanied the strike group up to a point just east of the island area. At that point, the strike group, led by the CO, proceeded farther north to a coast-in-point. Don and I broke off to the east and flew in to begin monitoring the fan-song radars on our shrike missiles. Only hitch here was that the ship had run out of shrikes, and there I was with only a load of bombs, in the worst SAM/flak area outside of Hanoi/Haiphong, with no passive radar to tell me when I was being tracked or painted by SAM or fire-control radar sites.

As the skipper rolled in, I got myself steeled somehow and flew in there like a madman, looking down gun barrels and directly at SAM sites known to be active, and went tearing into that area, found the SAM site that had fired on most of us, and laid my stick of bombs right across that momma. Bingo! Zap and away!

I was still in a hell of an area though and went dodging out the Haiphong channel at 2000 feet. Back at the ship, CAG and the skipper met me in the ready room, slapping me on the back and hollering congratulations. Tim cursed me properly because he and I have been plotting for a week on various ways to get up there and hit that particular site. After secure last night, we got a message from the admiral personally congratulating the two of us. Since Bost was leading the flight, he gets credit for my hit as well. Both of us are being recommended for Distinguished Flying Crosses for the flight.

September 6, 1966

Today I should have been with Marilyn for two days. Oh well, three days from now, we'll be in bed, and I'll be at home and content.

The moon is beautiful. For the first time this cruise the moon is out while our air group is flying. It takes more pressure off the flying groups than anything else could.

Yesterday we hit a train again and again, up there in the Nam Dinh area. Sure enough, you stir up a hornet's nest by repeating strike after strike. We stirred up a mess and got Capt. Allen shot down, and Ron brought back his plane full of holes.

All Ron saw was "something silver" behind him. Then he took a 37 mm cannon hit in his wing and a hit in the after portion of his cockpit. He brought his plane back, but it was touch-and-go all the way. He lost his radio immediately, or rather his transmitter, and couldn't tell anybody when Allen was lost. He didn't see Allen go in; Ron just missed him after being hit himself.

Ron couldn't get his wing up and finally came aboard, no radio, wing down, critically low fuel state, and broke his right main wheel upon landing. But he got back with no more injuries than bits of glass from the canopy imbedded in his forearms. And we have no idea what happened to Capt. Allen.

September 8, 1966

Today I was told that Chip will be my new wingman. Good deal. I think that Chip and I will both like that arrangement. Should make for some fun flights.

I'm completing a JAG report on Bob's accident so I won't have that hanging over me in port. Ah, but tomorrow night, I'll be holding Marilyn again. What sweetness!

September 23, 1966

We left Hong Kong this morning at 08:00. I left Marilyn at the hotel at about 05:15, caught a taxi with the skipper to the pier, and hired a walla-walla from there to the ship.

What can I say about the in-port period? Marilyn was there, and that made all the difference. Saying good-by to her was even more difficult than when we left San Diego.

September 27, 1966

Hurrah for the moon. It looks like it may be with us for the whole at-sea period. It's coming up in the afternoons now, and we're flying noon-to-midnight starting today. Along about the first of October, we'll be changing to midnight-to-noon, and the moon'll be just about caught up with us then, rising in the early hours of darkness.

I miss Marilyn already. Hell, I missed her when I walked out the door of our room in Hong Kong.

September 30, 1966

I've about had enough. I'm ready to get back home and set up my life with Marilyn and live like home folks.

I'm grounded again, sick with stomach cramps, fever, and chills. The skipper has the same thing. I had the duty yesterday and what misery. All night long I had had a fever and flew airplanes into the ground, into mountains, into the water, burning airplanes with no controls, black night flights with no instrument lights. I told the XO I could log seven hours of flight time for that night.

Day before yesterday Chip and I had some excitement. We were coming back from the islands. We still had three bullpup missiles, and I wanted to hit a group of boxcars I had seen parked off the railroad down north of Brandon Bay. As we were going south past Thanh Hoa, about ten miles to sea, I looked out and saw a big beautiful SAM joining up on us. I told Chip to hit the deck, and as we went roaring down from 10,000 feet, it went over us, still tracking, and exploded, shaking both airplanes. The second

SAM followed us down to 3000 feet and exploded close enough to put a hole in Chip's plane, or rather in his drop tank. Still not particularly excited, we went on down and shot the bullpups and knocked out the boxcars. We went around grinning at each other the rest of the day, and it was in that mood that I tried to write a poem, didn't make much sense, sort of about how alive you were when you weren't certain that you were going to be alive much longer.

When we landed and showed them where the missiles had come from, they launched a strike against the site, but no luck. They got the devil shot out of them, and Richard was thought to be shot down. But he turned up an hour or so later over the *Connie* with the nose of his airplane shot off completely. He landed on that carrier and came back yesterday, more than happy to be alive. A piece of flak came through the sole of his boot but didn't really hurt him. He said that he started to cut himself there with his knife to get a purple heart but changed his mind.

I'm flying in the morning. I'm not exactly well, but I'm not exactly sick either. I'm flying more because it's the biggest strike day for the whole at-sea period, and I don't want to miss it.

I've got the worst mission on the worst wave: Ironhand on the second wave. That means that the folks from the *Constellation* will stir them up like a hornet's nest, then we'll come in on the second wave when everybody's awake and at general quarters and all the MIG's are in the air, all the SAM's are up and ready, and there I'll sit at 10,000 feet with shrike missiles, looking for SAM's and just asking to be had.

Good old Chip! He had the duty tomorrow, and he traded with B-10 so he could go in with me.

I think I've been numb about Marilyn lately because I had so looked forward to seeing her in Manila and Hong Kong that I had thought of it as being the end of the cruise, and yet here I am again; she's gone, and I'm alone. All I've thought of today, however, is being with her, leading an orderly well-scheduled life, waking up with her there every morning, starting every day with her, touching her, knowing that she'll be there.

Two months now and we'll be together and, God willing, be together for a long time. I've been daydreaming all day about our taking a cabin cruiser up and down the inland waterway someday with kids age fifteen, thirteen, eleven, and so on. When the time comes, we're going to raise the most contrary, ugliest, meanest little hellions in the world, and I'm going to love and baby and cling to them.

October 2, 1966

The biggest thing to happen lately was a big "Wave" strike yesterday. All three carriers sent three Alpha strike-size groups in on one target, the Phu Ly complex of railroad yards, bridges, transhipment areas, and POL, on the railroad about ten miles south of Ko Tri bridge up around Nam Dinh. It was the biggest strike effort during the war I'm told. Starting at 07:15, the *Coral Sea* hit it with thirty-seven planes, then we hit at 07:45, then the *Connie* hit at 08:15, and so on throughout the day. Then we got up this morning and hit it twice again. Boy, that place must look like the moon!

But I didn't go on the strikes. I got up and briefed for it, went to the head and lost my breakfast, and was ordered to sick bay and told that I have a high fever. So I'm grounded.

October 4, 1966

No fly today; it's a stand-down. We start flying at midnight, but I don't have a hop until 06:00. I'm taking Chip out on a reconnaissance hop just to the south of Hanoi, so that should be fun. I'll get my reward when I get back. I get a test hop for the last hop of the day. That'll mean a full fuel tank, no ordnance, and I can raise hell for an hour and a half.

About our liberty port coming up in Japan; sorry about that. We were to have our last day on the line on the eleventh. It's been changed to the twenty-ninth. How's that? Just an extra eighteen days. Just double the time we were supposed to stay out here. The *Roosevelt* broke down completely, practically dead in the water. So she's going back to Japan for major repairs. Also the *Coral Sea* has to have a catapult overhauled. So who's to carry the load? You guessed it. When we left Hong Kong, one could say, "Only eighteen more days till in-port," but now he can only say, "With luck only twenty-five more days till in-port!" How about that!

Norris is the one who's bitter. He was scheduled to get out of the Navy and get off the boat in Japan. He still doesn't have separation orders and doesn't know when he's supposed to leave, even though his obligated time of service is finished. Without orders he can't do anything, can't ship his stuff home, move off base, ship his gear to Frisco, nothing.

Jack M. is gone to Denver. His girl already has them a house. He starts school for the airlines in December.

Thoughts like these are tearing through my mind like flashes from a slide projector: my first Christmas with Marilyn, snow on the ground, us running down a busy Christmas street holding hands, with flurries of snow dancing about us, a warm fire in some lost mountain lodge, a view of the hills and valley from the mountainside to the north of her folks' house with snow everywhere and only cars and trucks on the road, or cattle like her grandfather's, adding motion to the picture. And her there beside me, head on my shoulder . . . reasons for living.

October 6, 1966

I got a whole stack of letters today up to the first one Marilyn mailed from home. One letter was piss-poor. If Marilyn wants to preach of infidelity, unfaithfulness, and immorality, she should preach to the immoral, the unfaithful, and the infidels—not to me! Still, seeing so many married guys in the squadron running around with stray women in Hong Kong must weigh heavily on her mind, and I'm not going to write her a nasty letter: I'll just regret it if I do, like she is probably regretting her preaching right now.

It seems I spend more and more time daydreaming about going home and doing things with her this winter. I hope we can get a good house, one that is "outdoors," or lends itself to the out-of-doors.

I'm happy that she got the time in Japan and Hawaii. Don't know when the two of us will be able to make that trip together.

I just finished writing her and told her to ask her Daddy to lend us his pickup truck in December to take to the drive-in movie. I hope it doesn't have a heater. I'd sure like to be cuddled up next to her in some cold, frosty drive-in eating popcorn and watching Randolph Scott tame the West. And in an old truck, it sounds so North Carolina I can't think of anything any more attractive.

I'm feeling much better and flying again. Marilyn said that she was sick with the same thing. We must have eaten too much coconut oil or something. I know what she means about "single married life"; I keep reaching out for her and get disappointed every time.

October 9, 1966

Haven't written in the last three days, but it seems I've just got some bug that won't leggo. I'm not grounded or really sick, but I just feel rotten all the time, run-down and tired.

Day before yesterday I had a day hop with Steve; went up around Thanh Hoa without much resistance. Yesterday Chip and I went up around Thanh Hoa and didn't really get anything done. And again at midnight, I took Jerry out for a worthless hop above Brandon Bay. Then, for the first time in about a week, I got eight hours sleep all at once, in a row, undisturbed. And I feel like a new person; a tired new person, run-down, but still newer than before.

Today while I slept, there was real action going on; covering a strike of Phu Ly, Joe and Ed were jumped by MIG-21's (the advanced MIG, comparable in performance to our F-4's). The F-8's were already on the way, but Ed had a rough time getting away from one of the MIG's. Cdr. Bell, the hero of the day, shot down one of the MIG's and was immediately hustled away to Saigon for a debriefing by the big brass. An F-4 from the *Roosevelt* was shot down, and while the rescue operation was going on, the MIG's jumped the spads flying RESCAP. With exceeding skill and daring and one hell of a lot of luck, one of the spads sprayed one of the MIG's with 20 mm and shot him down! How about that! We hadn't shot a MIG down the whole cruise, and no sooner does one of our fighter pilots shoot one down, than he's outdone by a prop pilot from another ship. *C'est la guerre.*

Yesterday, one of our spad pilots, Harold Bishop, a third tour lieutenant was shot down by automatic weapons over in the back country. His wingman was shot up pretty bad but got back okay. Harold probably went in with his plane.

I may be interviewed for CBS TV later for my strike on the SAM site. They probably want to prove to the American public that the average fighting man here is a homegrown country hick. I've heard my voice on tape. Amazing, that a man with the things I have to say should be blessed with such a corn-fed voice.

Beautiful letters from Marilyn today. Do I ever miss her! I miss her at the dinner table, beside me in the car, walking with her, and being a simple, sensual being rooted in the physical, I miss the hell out of her in bed.

I think Christmas is certainly dragging its feet this year. I thought at about age twenty-one that Christmas was something I had forgotten how to anticipate with the eagerness of a child. But not so this year. Never before has Christmas meant so much. Also, Thanksgiving Day will have a more special meaning to me this year; my blessings have so multiplied. The year of our Lord, Nineteen Hundred and Sixty-Six, the year of awakened senses of gain and loss, pain and joy, togetherness and parting, anticipation, disappointment, unexpected and undeserved joy, love, hope, the year of combat and its associated terrors, the year of our Lord, Nineteen Hundred and Sixty-Six, *The Year of Marilyn*.

October 10, 1966

This midnight-to-noon routine is killing. Really killing. We only seem to heckle the enemy and keep him awake and maybe make him keep his lights off at night, but we fly airplanes into the ground, into mountains, into the sea and lose sleep because nobody can get used to going to bed at noon. I'm getting sick of the whole affair. Still I try to remember that I asked to be here.

Just in the last week or so, the antiaircraft defenses seem to have doubled or tripled, and you get shot at now from places where even a month or so ago you could overfly with relative security. We've lost 10 per cent of our pilots and 20 per cent of our aircraft on this cruise so far, and we're not on our way home yet.

With luck, I'll make it home for Christmas.

October 11, 1966

Wahoo, hurrah, and yippee! We're off the mid-to-noon for a whole week. Now it's noon-to-midnight, and that's so sweet it's like a chance to fly other than completely exhausted.

Sign on the ready room chalkboard: "Only 30 more Bombing Days till Christmas, get yours done early!" Sign number 2: "Flight Surgeon Sez: Get your annual physical. Those not complying will be grounded (upon arrival in San Diego)!" Sign number 3: "Yossarian Sez: The Ironhand that was scheduled to be cancelled will brief 30 minutes early."

Night before last I took B-10 out on a night bombing hop and found and bombed a convoy of trucks. Stumbled around for twenty minutes not knowing where the devil we were, getting shot at from everywhere, looking for checkpoint 38. Finally gave up and decided to go out and get oriented and find something else. Heading out, I saw two lights, dropped two flares to mark the spot, and found the convoy.

On a later hop yesterday, I took Jerry out and scared the devil out of us both. I led him through a couple of double-Immelmans, stalling out over the top of each one. Then I did some zero-airspeed, hammerhead climbs that always scare me. But then I did the grand finale which I never admitted to him that I had never had the guts to try before; I let down to low altitude over the water, getting lower and lower, 100 feet, then 50, then 20, then 10. Then finally I let my hook down and eased it down till the hook touched the water twice, and that was at about 350 knots. Great fun! I took Barry out today and did the same thing; but Barry did it too. I not only never did it before; I never heard of anyone's doing it. And when I saw Barry's hook touch the water, I decided that maybe I'd never try it again. When your hook hits, your drop tank is only about eighteen inches above the water.

It seems that we never go into AI in the morning anymore but what there's another report of a Navy pilot downed. Just every day. Just count them off.

But now, glorious day, we're off the mid-to-noon for a week.

Night before last after I wrote Marilyn, while I was lying in bed for that six hours, I lay there and hated that night hop and hated that night hop and hated the strain of flying where you have to look in every direction at once and look out for yourself and somebody else and hated the Navy and mostly hated that doggoned night hop and the fact that I couldn't go to sleep so long that the very idea of a whole career in the Navy was so remote to me that I decided that I wanted out of all this, decided that the thing for me to do was go through three years of shore duty and then go back to North Carolina and do something: law, teach, anything, start a business, run the farm, and get out of all this. As far as that period of tossing and turning, rolling, forcing myself to lie still while I took first one hundred deep breaths in one position and one hundred deep breaths in another position in an effort to make my body go to sleep, as far as that four hours went, it was certain that the only thing for me to do was to get out. I thought of all the times when I was growing up, even in high school, that I was afraid of something and took the easy way out, of all the times I was scared and took the coward's way out, of all the times I didn't think I could look the other guys in the face and feel that I was quite the same stuff they were, fights I backed down from, loafing at football practice, loafing on the farm sometimes, or not putting everything I had into any one of a thousand things. I could think of all that, knowing that if I turned in my wings, that I'd have to live all my life in that same feeling of shame, having the medals but secretly knowing that I had given up because I didn't think I had the stuff to keep going when it got rough. And yet, it wasn't quite enough.

I had all that on the one hand, and on the other hand was that damned night hop coming up in the ink black that seems to belong exclusively to the night over here, the uncertainty that the airplane was going to make it into the air off the cat, the terror of not knowing—or of having to find—the exact right spot to coast in, of having to watch out not only for myself but to coordinate and control, to maintain order, to keep track of that all-important wingman, and to get back and find the ship and make sure that he got back and got aboard, and then to fly that ink-black approach and not break my neck on the ramp or fly into the water or fly into the sea or into a mountain or into the ground and see to it that my wingman didn't.

All these things can be done easily enough taken one thing at a time, but lying in bed knowing that you'll be required to do it all, it all lies on your mind at once, and you can't sleep and every minute goes by and you know that that's one minute more of precious sleep you lost and need to be safe and get the job done safely and yet you can't sleep and you just lie there and lie there and you can't stop thinking about it all and you toss and it never quits.

It would almost be a relief to get up right then and brief and go and do it all, but you can't even do that; you just lie there knowing that when it's really time to go that then you'll be sleepy and tired out and unsafe, and there's nothing, absolutely nothing, you can do about it. It's horrible. And it happens every night, every night until you're off that awful schedule.

And now we're off that schedule for a week. The feeling of relief is inexpressible. Now I can know that although it'll be night flying and Vinh and Nam Dinh and Cam Pha and Haiphong and all the rest, it'll be a schedule on which I face things one at a time, doing each thing as it becomes necessary, living one day at a time, and getting enough sleep and

rest to do it sanely and as safely and as much under control as possible.

Still in the back of my mind is the knowledge that sooner or later, a week, eight days, ten, and we'll be back on it again. That's what I came to find out: whether it was really just in my mind, or if I could really hack a combat flying billet, and what it was really like. So now I know. To tell the truth it's about what I expected—harder'n hell.

Scott and I had a discussion once. We're pretty honest with each other, and the subject of his having to prove himself to himself all the time and my having to do the same thing came up. I remember his laughing once and saying something like, "Well, it's true, I don't believe in myself enough to just say, 'Now Scott, you can do as much or more than anybody else and you don't have to prove a thing,' I've got to show myself." And then he said, "But dammit I do show myself, and do prove things to me and as long as I can keep doing things other folks can't do and things I don't really believe I can do, where's the harm except in the fact that someday I'll fail to prove something—and I've done that before too—where's the hurt if I manage to successfully prove myself?" And I guess that's me over here.

I hate night hops, but almost only when they're the first hop of the day. And every time I walk up on that deck knowing what's coming up, it's like facing death. Hell, more than that, it is facing death; but I think I face it sometimes more heavy-hearted than other folks. I think I'm sometimes more cowardly about it than others, more hesitant. But dammit, I do it. So where's the hurt as long as I manage to get it done?

My Darling Marilyn,

I don't really have time to write a decent letter, but I just received your letters, and I wanted to write a thank you note. Or better, an I love you and am thankful for you note. I do and I am.

I'm sitting here in the room eating gee dunk because I didn't feel like getting dressed and then back into flight gear. That's because Robert McNamara, General Wheeler, and a bunch of other admirals and Army generals and captains and colonels are aboard for the night.

The captain came over the intercom today and said, "Now we're just going to show them a normal day's operation," and now the aviator's chow line is closed.

I missed the big action this morning. Down to the south, Darell was hitting a truck park and was using his bomb computer. The computer fouled up and threw a bomb out into the boonies, and they got all sorts of gigantic secondary explosions. So everyone kept bombing that area and kept getting fires and explosions. It was probably a stockpile area for the DMZ forces. The next three launches were diverted into that area and got all kinds of results. Really a big day. I missed it all. My hop was traded with Joe so that he could escort the VIP's tonight, and I got a tanker hop which aborted. I didn't care; I'd rather give up the hop than do that escort duty.

Another bit of excitement occurred today when a number of motorized craft resembling PT boats were approaching the ship's steaming area from the north. We all figured that maybe we'd get some antisurface action, but they turned out to be Chinese motorized fishing trawlers. The *Constellation* found them first and was all set to sink them when pictures revealed that the single gun mount on the bow was really a crane.

Another A-D pilot down back in the woods. One a day.

I read and read again and again the things you said about the autumn, and it sounded so good I couldn't stop thinking about it. You can't know how much I wish I were there. Won't be long. Even so it seems so long. Tick-tick. It seems like a million years since I saw you last.

I'm looking forward to our cross-country trip to California. Maybe we can borrow sleeping bags and camp out a couple of nights. I love you so much I don't think we'd need but one sleeping bag or even use the other one if we had two.

Well, brief time for my flight. Taking Chip out again tonight. All my love, darling, and thank you again for your lovely thoughts in those two letters today.

I love you.
Frank

WESTERN UNION TELEGRAM

TO: Mrs. Frank Callihan Elkins, Route One, Dunlap, Tennessee

I deeply regret to confirm on behalf of the United States Navy that your husband, Lt. Frank Callihan Elkins, 658100/1310, USN is missing in action. This occurred on 13 October 1966 while on a combat mission over North Vietnam. It is believed your husband was maneuvering his aircraft to avoid hostile fire when radio contact was lost. An explosion was observed but it could not be determined whether this was hostile fire exploding or your husband's aircraft. No parachute or visual signals were observed and no emergency radio signals were received. You may be assured that every effort is being made with personnel and facilities available to locate your husband. Your great anxiety in this situation is understood and when further information is available concerning the results of the search now in progress you will be promptly notified. I join you in fervent hope for his eventual recovery alive. I wish to assure you of every possible assistance together with the heartfelt sympathy of myself and your husband's shipmates at this time of heartache and uncertainty.

The area in which your husband became missing presents the possibility that he could be held by hostile force against his will. Accordingly, for his safety in this event, it is suggested that in replying to inquiries from sources outside your immediate family you reveal only his name, rank, file number, and date of birth.

Vice Admiral B. J. Semmes, Jr.
Chief of Naval Personnel

Epilogue

Soon after the 1973 publication of Frank's diary, I left Paris for San Francisco and began a career in business. The Navy continued to send me official communications describing the U.S. government's ongoing efforts on Frank's behalf. The current president mailed me an annual Christmas card with a letter affirming his efforts to obtain information about Frank. And finally on Halloween in 1977—in what I now interpret as one of a rather unfortunate series of coincidences regarding dates—the Navy sent me a telegram that officially changed Frank's status to a Presumed Finding of Death (PFOD). Yet even this official communication used the words "presumed" and "assumed."

But this announcement prompted Frank's family and me

to hold a memorial service for him in the National Cemetery in Wilmington, North Carolina. At the time I thought that event concluded his life, giving our families and me the only closure that we could hope for. Occasionally Frank's mother mentioned that she still felt he might be alive, but I assumed that he was not and tried to accept his life and death as being complete.

Throughout the rest of the seventies, I lived in San Francisco, hoping to avoid anything that reminded me of my earlier life with Frank. But controlling dreams is impossible. I kept encountering different versions of the same one. A combination of the past and a kind of never-to-be future, it always began with Frank calling me to say that he was on his way home.

"Will you meet me?"

"Of course!"

I'd arrive at the agreed-upon destination (it varied from dream to dream) only to find I had arrived too late and must now meet him in some other, more-difficult-to-find location. This sequence of failed connections continued until I finally gave up from despair and exhaustion. And while I continued to search, I would hear Frank repeating something he had actually said to me on one of our first dates: "Don't act dumb. If I wanted a dumb woman, I would look for one." I'd usually awake from such dreams crying, angry at my own inability to negotiate the necessary labyrinth to find him. And I would once again resolve to forget "all that" and get on with my life.

Eventually, however, I admitted that forgetting my interest in literature and teaching—an interest that I had forsaken because it was one that Frank and I had shared—was also impossible. This realization prompted my move, in 1981, to New Orleans to teach English at a public high school for the gifted. My students were challenging, and I slowly re-discovered the pleasures that I continue to receive from reading and writing.

Frank and I had also shared a plan to earn our Ph.D.'s in English and become college professors. After spending a summer in New York at Columbia and a fall sabbatical at Georgetown, I finally admitted that I still wanted to pursue that goal. What I had been dismissing as Frank's road map for our lives was also what I wanted, with or without him.

In the fall of 1987, I enrolled in the English Ph.D. program at the University of North Carolina at Chapel Hill. Although it had not been a factor in my decision, the location did allow me to re-establish my closeness with Frank's family. And in some ways that association has been the most rewarding aspect of the past three years.

Absorbed in my graduate work, I rarely wondered if I would receive additional information about Frank's whereabouts. Twelve silent years after his being declared a PFOD, in December of 1989, Lt. David Oswald of the Navy's POW/MIA Affairs division called to ask if I "happened to have" a copy of my husband's dental x-rays.

"No . . . why?"

"Well . . . uh . . . we have a piece of a jawbone and some teeth that we think may have belonged to him."

My anger at Oswald's unfeeling language obscured my initial shock. How could this stranger choose his words so carelessly, ignoring their possible effect upon me? But his tone of voice indicated that he was not so unfeeling as his word choice implied. He explained that Frank was only one of several men who were being considered as the possible source for a box of remains that the North Vietnamese had turned over to American authorities in June. I suggested that Lt. Oswald contact my husband's family to see if they could provide him with the name of Frank's childhood dentist. As I had during the past twenty-three years, I tried to remain calm when confronted with unexpected reminders of Frank and of my own, irretrievable loss.

On 22 January 1990, Frank's and my twenty-fourth wedding anniversary, I returned from a day on campus to find an answering-machine message asking that I call Lt. Oswald at home. As usual, I was aware of our wedding anniversary. And hoping to avoid more unfortunate coincidences (after all Frank's plane was shot down on my mother's birthday, and Barry Bridger, Frank's best man, was shot down over North Vietnam exactly one year after he had been in our wedding), I hesitated to return Lt. Oswald's call. Instead, I phoned friends, casually mentioning the call to see what advice they might give. Finally having gathered the necessary courage, I called Lt. Oswald. He informed me that members of the government's repatriation team had identified the remains as Frank's.

The Navy's terms for what was to follow still strike me as bizarre. Frank's remains would be "repatriated" after the records of this initial identification work had been perused by three independent forensic pathologists. If the pathologists agreed with the findings, Lt. Oswald and John Rogers, the director of the Navy's Decedent/Mortuary Affairs Program, would fly to Chapel Hill to explain exactly how these records "proved" that the bones belonged to Frank. (The bones included those of the torso, legs, and a part of the lower jawbone that seemed to be broken. No bones were available from the rest of the face and head or the feet and hands.) If I found the pathologists' reports "inconclusive," I would have the "option" to arrange for someone else to review the paperwork and remains to provide "quality assurance" of this decision.

A few days later, Colonel Walls and Master Chief Edwards of the UNC–Chapel Hill NROTC department came by and offered their assistance, promising to help me make any necessary arrangements. Both men seemed unusually kind and thoughtful, and I found their local presence somehow reassuring. But while I waited, nothing seemed reassuring enough. I spent the next few weeks alternating between fears that the pathologists would agree that these remains belonged to Frank and that they would not. And this limbo, this waiting, was altogether too like my earlier waiting for Frank to come walking—unharmed— out of the jungle. If you've spent eleven years of your life married to someone who is officially listed as missing in action, any delay seems unusually difficult to bear.

The additional pressures of my academic life intensified my anxiety. I was experiencing Frank's loss again in a very emotional way, yet none of my students, and only a few friends, knew about these events. I vacillated between wanting everyone to know—hoping that they would excuse my distracted behavior—and wanting to be so strong that no one would guess I was under any unusual stress. On some level I was unsure of people's reaction; during the Vietnam war, I had often encountered unsympathetic responses to my situation.

And while I still couldn't be sure that the pathologists would decide the bones belonged to Frank, I could be sure that I was terrified about going through the ordeal of understanding how they had reached their decision. I was also afraid that I might become physically ill because of the emotions I was experiencing. I kept remembering the 1966 Christmas after Frank's disappearance over Vietnam, the only time I have ever been hospitalized for my Crohn's disease, a chronic ailment that seems to be exacerbated by stress.

Part of me wanted to refuse to participate in this identification process and just let the Navy decide what to do with those bones. And while my earlier dream of looking for Frank did not return, almost every night I would awaken with a line from Toni Morrison's novel *Song of Solomon* going through my head: "You just can't fly off and leave a body." Of course, I knew that. But asking me to go through the upcoming ordeal seemed unfair. Hadn't this insane war already cost me enough pain? Why did I have to go through this ridiculous twenty-three-years-too-late mourning process?

Resenting my seemingly uncontrollable sleeplessness, I became angry at Frank and the Navy for what I—in my self-preservation mode—considered their absolutely horrible insistence on following Navy procedures. I desperately wanted to stay on track with my own schedule to complete my degree. Selfishly, I kept focusing on how poorly timed this whole event was, managing to allow some of my emotional response to be subsumed by these mundane concerns. And I couldn't even decide what I really wanted: part of me seemed to prefer that Frank's death remain unsubstantiated.

Fortunately, the pathologists concurred quickly that the remains were Frank's. On 13 February 1990 Oswald, Rogers, and Walls met with me to explain how the Navy had reached its decision. Frank's niece and nephew, who also live in Chapel Hill, generously volunteered to be present with me during this meeting. The process was painful, and although these people did everything that they could to help make it less so, it remains almost as upsetting a memory as my initial receipt of the 1966 telegram.

Lieutenant Oswald and John Rogers explained that the government research group reached their decision based upon a combination of evidence. First they looked for the names of all of the men who were listed as having disappeared in the area of Dien Chau District, Nghe Tinh Province—the area from which the bones had been recovered. Using a section of the pelvic bone to determine the age of the person at death, they were able to narrow the possibilities even more. By measuring the torso and leg bones, they were also able to estimate the person's height. Because of the prominent muscle insertion in the bones, the pathologists were certain that the person had an unusually muscular build; Frank's medical records show that he had a 42" chest, 31" waist, and 22" thigh and could military press 200 pounds; he had begun lifting weights when he was in high school, an activity that he continued. Using information from the computer data base of missing person's dental records, they narrowed the possibilities to three men. And while they were able to obtain dental x-rays on all of these men except Frank, none of their x-rays fit the dental work remaining on the lower jawbone. Although no x-rays of Frank's teeth were available, the dental charts showing his fillings and earlier extractions matched those of the jawbone. So he fit the description in every possible way, as did no one else who had disappeared within a fifty-mile radius of the site.

With the recounting of each explanation, I was asked if I wanted to see photographs of the bones or medical records that substantiated each claim. At first I could only respond "I don't know yet. Wait a minute, and I'll let you know." And then I would tell myself that I had to look or continue to doubt their judgment. Each decision to look at the evidence became a little easier, and I managed to get through the afternoon without embarrassing any of us by becoming hysterical. Steven and Susan told me later that if I had not agreed to look at the photographs they would have done so since they also felt we needed to look to be able to know.

Frank appears to have died in the crash of his plane. The fragmentation of the bones and the broken jaw make this the most likely explanation. The bones were encrusted with dirt since the Vietnamese bury them directly in the ground without a coffin and then, approximately three years later, after the flesh has rotted away, dig them up and place them in a smaller grave. This process also partly accounts for the missing smaller bones. When this ritual was explained to me, it was described as something that the Vietnamese do because of their "superstitions" about the dead. I couldn't help thinking that we characterize our own practices, really no more civilized, about such matters as "respect for the dead."

Using negative words to describe the customs of people who are not American helps us justify our harsh treatment and assessment of them. But I am touched that the Vietnamese went to such trouble to bury someone who had been bombing their country. Their humane customs are partly responsible for my having Frank's remains for reburial. And I was beginning to discover how grateful I was. But now I had to decide what to do with those remains. They would be shipped to Travis Air Force Base and brought home to North Carolina in late February, and I began to plan a private, quiet interment in the National Cemetery in Wilmington.

When Frank was listed as missing in action, I had appeared on television and radio and given countless newspaper interviews hoping to call public attention to the MIA/POW plight. But publicity could no longer help Frank. And now that his death was final, I wanted a private funeral without curiosity seekers. I also knew from our conversations that Frank would want the ceremony to be as simple as possible. When I warned Frank's family that we would have difficulty keeping his burial a private occasion, they, unselfishly, promised to handle calls from the media.

With the Navy's help, I was able to get Frank's favorite nephew home from Germany to serve as the military escort for the remains from California to North Carolina. Colonel Walls arranged for the cemetery to be closed to everyone but family and friends, and we managed to get inside the gates without an incident. But a reporter from a Wilmington newspaper climbed an adjacent hill and using a zoom lens took photographs, despite our careful planning. Sitting next to me, my brother noticed the woman during the service, but said nothing for fear of upsetting me. So I did not know that we were being photographed when the Navy escort folded the flag from the coffin and presented it to me. When I saw the newspaper the next day, I was furious.

I had talked with the chaplain at length, and I liked the brief address that he gave. At my suggestion, he read the Robert Frost poem that appears in this book. When the bugler played taps, a suggestion that Colonel Walls made and for which I am grateful, I realized just how appropriate that traditional closing is for a military ceremony. And I began to sense how different this ceremony was for me from the earlier memorial that we had held.

After the ceremony, a number of Frank's friends, some of whom I had not seen for years, came by to talk. I was moved by their remembering him and caring enough to make the trip to Wilmington for his funeral. And I was pleased that so many members of our families attended. Their presence made me feel less alone in continuing to care about Frank.

Later that night my sister-in-law and I stayed awake talking about Frank and my own experiences in relation to his death. For years I had maintained that since Frank was dead, the location of his body was insignificant. I had been lying to myself, diminishing the importance of what I could not change. I had never before spent a night openly crying about his death in the presence of someone else. Expressing my grief had seemed indulgent and disloyal as long as Frank was listed as missing in action. And his "presumed" death seemed just one more formality, another step in my diminution of hope, but somehow not complete or sure. It lacked the finality of this event, and perhaps I had subconsciously continued to hope that Frank might return.

But that is changing. Knowing the whereabouts of Frank's remains has become absolutely crucial to that process. On the morning following his interment, I returned to the grave site alone. After a sleepless night spent crying, I was just swollen-eyed and punchy enough to stand without self-consciousness for a long time and study the landscape, particularly the tall, full oaks that are silhouetted against the sky. Although Frank is dead and obviously cannot see those trees, I find their presence above his grave comforting. Unlike the young slain soldier in Thomas Hardy's poem "Drummer Hodge," Frank no longer rests "uncoffined" beneath "foreign constellations." The solace I receive from being able to call up that familiar sky continues to be important to me.

As does my relief at knowing that I've completed the role I feel Frank's wife should have played. Somehow I believed that I had failed him by being unable to find his body and bring it home. Knowing rationally how unrealistic such guilt is does little to diminish its force. His burial frees me from the feeling of having deserted someone I love. What started out as irritating—because it took up so much time and energy—and painful—because it called up such deep emotions—has become a powerful, internal healing for me.

Yet finding any justifiable reason for Frank's death remains problematic for me. It seems worthwhile only for its confirmation of his belief in himself, in his courage to die for what he perceived as national duty. But his death did not help anyone else.

Perhaps his diary can. Perhaps it can serve as a permanent example of the personal cost of wars in American life, since as a nation we often seem unmoved by the deaths of those equally good people who are not American. Perhaps it can also be part of the accumulating evidence that such wars—those fought on foreign soils over other people's decisions about *their* destinies—can rarely be just or worthwhile. And perhaps this epilogue can broaden the awareness of war's impact on those who are forced to participate vicariously through the people they choose to love. But I am forced to preface each of these suppositions with "perhaps."

Such hopes offer a damned small consolation. Yet like the return of Frank's remains twenty-three years after his death, even that cold comfort seems a miracle.

—*Marilyn Elkins*

Frank Callihan Elkins was a native of Bladenboro, North Carolina, where he was high-school quarterback and valedictorian. He earned his B.A. in English from the University of North Carolina at Chapel Hill and entered the U.S. Navy and flight training in 1961. He married Marilyn Roberson in January of 1966. After the crash of his A-4 Skyhawk over Vietnam on October 13, 1966, he was listed as missing in action until 1977. He was awarded seven air medals and the Distinguished Flying Cross. In January of 1990, his remains were identified and returned.

The **Naval Institute Press** is the book-publishing arm of the U.S. Naval Institute, a private, nonprofit professional society for members of the sea services and civilians who share an interest in naval and maritime affairs. Established in 1873 at the U.S. Naval Academy in Annapolis, Maryland, where its offices remain today, the Naval Institute has more than 100,000 members worldwide.

Members of the Naval Institute receive the influential monthly magazine *Proceedings* and discounts on fine nautical prints, ship and aircraft photos, and subscriptions to the quarterly *Naval History* magazine. They also have access to the transcripts of the Institute's Oral History Program and get discounted admission to any of the Institute-sponsored seminars regularly offered around the country.

The Naval Institute's book-publishing program, begun in 1898 with basic guides to naval practices, has broadened its scope in recent years to include books of more general interest. Now the Naval Institute Press publishes more than forty new titles each year, ranging from how-to books on boating and navigation to battle histories, biographies, ship and aircraft guides, and novels. Institute members receive discounts on the Press's more than 375 books.

Full-time students are eligible for special half-price membership rates. Life memberships are also available.

For a free catalog describing the Naval Institute Press books currently available, and for further information about U.S. Naval Institute membership, please write to:

Membership & Communications Department
U.S. Naval Institute
Annapolis, Maryland 21402

Or call, toll-free, (800) 233-USNI. In Maryland, call (301) 224-3378.

THE NAVAL INSTITUTE PRESS

THE HEART OF A MAN

A Naval Pilot's Vietnam Diary

Designed by Pamela L. Schnitter

Set in Sabon and Mistral
by TCSystems, Inc.
Shippensburg, Pennsylvania

Printed on 55-lb. Warren Sebago Cream-White
and bound in Holliston Kingston Natural
by R.R. Donnelley & Sons Company
Harrisonburg, Virginia